ORGANISATIONAL DESIGN

Organisational Design

The Work-Levels Approach

Ralph Rowbottom
and
David Billis

Gower

Aldershot · Brookfield USA · Hong Kong · Singapore · Sydney

Published by
Gower Publishing Company Limited
Gower House
Croft Road
Aldershot
Hants GU11 3HR
England

Gower Publishing Company
Old Post Road
Brookfield
Vermont 05036
USA

British Library Cataloguing in Publication Data

Rowbottom, Ralph
 Organisational design : the work-levels
 approach.
 1. Organisation
 I. Title   II. Billis, David
 302.3′5   HD31

Library of Congress Cataloging-in-Publication Data

Rowbottom, Ralph William
 Organisational design.

 Includes bibliographies and index.
 1. Delegation of authority.   2. Organisation.
I. Billis, David.   II. Title.
HD50.R68   1987   658.4′02   86–31946

Printed in Great Britain at the
University Press, Cambridge
ISBN 0 566 05408 6

Contents

Acknowledgements

Our prime thanks go to our colleagues as a whole in the Brunel Institute of Organisation and Social Studies from whom we have drawn so much both at the level of detailed formulations and broader philosophies. Our specific debt to the ideas of Elliott Jaques is obvious, and warmly acknowledged. We are grateful to Warren Kinston for his substantial comments on the content and drafting. And we thank Zena Pereira for her invaluable help with the material production.

PART ONE
THE GENERAL
APPROACH

1 Introduction

'It's impossible to get clear decisions made.' 'There's no proper direction or policy, no systematic planning or development.' 'Costs are not under adequate control.' 'There's not enough scope for individual initiative.' 'You don't get enough personal support and guidance.' 'Communication is poor.' 'There's no real consultation.' 'Teams don't function properly.' 'Delegation is in name only.' 'Overall, it's far too bureaucratic.'

In twenty years of work in a wide variety of organisations we have heard such complaints time and time again. They have come up in factories, banks, insurance companies, hospitals, schools and welfare agencies. They have emerged equally in discussions at top, middle and shop-floor levels. They have been voiced by front-line workers and managers, professionals and administrators, operational staff and support workers. Sometimes investigation has shown that the difficulties are caused, or at least exacerbated, by particular people: by an inadequate individual here or an awkward personality there. But usually, it turns out, the problem is deeper: it resides in the basic structure itself.

In this book we describe an approach to organisational design that has grown from helping people in a wide variety of settings to grapple with basic problems of just these kinds. In carrying out such work it often becomes apparent in fact that one of the first things wrong is classic: people simply do not know how much authority and respons-ibility they have. Foremen wonder whether or not they are genuine 'first-line managers'. More-senior production staff complain of undue interference from specialists and headquarters people. Ward sisters are left unsure of the extent of their control over night-nursing. Social-work team leaders are not clear how far they are responsible for the work of other team members. Regional officers in banking or insurance find that local managers regularly bypass them in dealings with headquarters. The exact powers of designated deputies and assistants are often a matter of considerable doubt and controversy.

Frequently, official charts and job descriptions compound rather than resolve the difficulties. Does the fact that A is shown higher than B on the chart mean that the first is a clear 'boss'? Or does it merely indicate that he or she is paid more? Or does it mean (yet again) that he or she does indeed have some authority over B, but not that of a straightforward boss or manager?

In trying to resolve such issues the notion of 'line and staff' is sometimes advanced. However it is usually of little practical help, if not positively misleading. It is readily demonstrable that relations in large organisations do *not* fall into two simple categories: the one, 'line', involving authority to instruct; and the other 'staff', authority only to influence or advise. All sorts of other possibilities evidently exist in various combinations: powers to monitor, powers to report upon, powers to co-ordinate, powers to prescribe detailed tasks and methods, an so on. ('Unity of command' – the idea that all instructions should come down one line only – turns out, too, to be a largely misleading principle.)

Often, then, the first things to be dealt with in tackling problems of the kind described earlier are unclear authority relations, and the way in which authority is confused with differential pay or grading. But as these are gradually sorted out, as the key managerial roles are separated from other types, a fresh range of issues is revealed. Just how many or few main management levels can any given organisation in fact support? Is ten too many, fifteen, or even twenty? Would five or even less be too few? (And how would this relate to spans of control?) Does a small organisation need as many levels as a big one? If not, what do terms like 'top', 'middle' and 'first-line' management really mean, and how does the essential quality of work change from one to another? Why is it, for example, that most sales representatives appear to be doing much more responsible work than most production workers, even though both are shown on the bottom rung of the organisational ladder? Why is it that doctors are regarded as more senior than, say, physiotherapists, and the latter more senior than hospital porters, even though all work directly with patients? Most fundamentally of all, how do, or should, elaborate structures of management and organisation relate to the work at the front line: the services actually delivered to the individual customer or client?

The Work-Level Theory
What has emerged from our own exploration of these and similar questions is a fundamental theory of *work levels*, a theory which seems to have application to a very wide range of jobs and activities in

organisations both large and small. The detailed description of this theory must be left until later pages, but suffice it to say at this point that it involves essentially the identification of a range of different responses that an organisation or any of its constituent parts can be expected to make to its environment, each increasingly more complex, penetrating, and comprehensive, as level succeeds level.

Given a general theory of work levels it becomes possible to make much more specific pronouncements about structural design: about how many main management levels are needed, about the exact kind or level of impact on customers or clients required at the operational front line, about the different sorts of output or response expected in all other jobs. Building on such a theory, it also becomes possible to take a new look at the personal dimension: at how individuals differ not just in basic personality or special areas of skill, but in terms of ability to operate at any given level; and how, moreover, such abilities change and develop for each individual during the course of his or her working life. It becomes possible to indicate just what sort of support and guidance should be provided for staff at various levels; and, conversely, just how much room should be left for each to exercise his or her own particular powers of judgement and initiative. It becomes possible to construct much more effective channels of communication, up and down; and to be much clearer about how staff at various levels can realistically participate in higher executive management. It becomes possible to see much better how different sorts of team need to operate and how various prospects for decentralisation can be effectively realised.

The Form of the Book
As just described, the exploration of problems as they are actually experienced in a wide range of different organisations has led us and our colleagues over the years to more detailed and realistic conceptions of authority relationships than are commonly in use. Beyond this it has led to the development of a fundamental theory of work levels. And, associated with the last, it has led to a radically different conception of individual abilities and the way they change through working life. Taken together, these three sets of ideas on (a) different types of *authority relationships*, (b) different *levels of work*, and (c) different *levels of individual ability*, provide an approach to organisational design of considerable power and scope. The approach does not pretend to address, let alone to resolve, every issue of organisation – it does not for example, go deeply into the whole question of governance and governing bodies. But the range of applications is nevertheless wide.

The chapters which follow describe first the general ideas themselves and then how they apply to specific fields. Part One shows in effect how the general design approach necessarily proceeds if problems of the kind described earlier are to be fundamentally resolved. We start with the basic distinction between grading structures and management structures, and then examine the varieties of distinct roles – well beyond the simple dichotomy of 'line' and 'staff' – that must be recognised in the design of the latter. We expound the general theory of work levels which underlies management structures and examine the relationship between the two. We see where actual people come in, by considering how individual abilities relate to required levels of work, and what this means for appraisal, career development, and reward. We summarise six prime design issues: the *basic level of work output required* from any organisation, the *highest level of work output required*, the *number of main management levels required*, the *optimum grouping of activities* at each, *dealing with excessive spans of control*, and *necessary staff and support structure*. Finally, we consider the implications of the ideas for a variety of further organisational issues including teamwork, matrix organisation, decentralisation, and various schemes for enhancing worker participation.

Part Two describes how the approach applies to particular fields and settings. A considerable range of practical experience has now been amassed. The approach has been discussed and developed in a stream of workshops and seminars that has been running at the Institute of Organisation and Social Studies at Brunel University for the last fifteen years or so, attended by thousands of senior staff from industry, commerce, voluntary agencies, the civil service, local government, the health service and other public agencies throughout Britain. It has been used in projects and discussions in ICI, Alcan, Hoover, and Plessey; in special conferences mounted for two insurance companies, Commercial Union and Prudential; and in workshops run in India for the Ahmedabad Textile Industry Research Association. It has been employed in major organisational developments in many Health Authorities, including those in Exeter, Newcastle, Nottingham and York; and in many Local Authority Social Services including those in Brent, Derbyshire, Leicestershire, Norfolk, North Tyneside, and Wandsworth. It has been used in developments sponsored by several professional associations, including the Royal College of Psychiatry, the Chartered Society of Physiotherapists, and the Clinical Psychology Division of the British Psychological Society. It has been employed in projects in a number of voluntary agencies including MIND, Mencap, the Volunteer Centre, and the Notting Hill Housing Association. Its relevance to various

European settings has been discussed in workshops run for the United Nations Social Welfare Centre. (Various accounts have already been published by ourselves and colleagues of applications in many of these latter public and voluntary service areas.[1])

Drawing on all this experience, the various chapters of Part Two summarise how the approach applies to factory organisation; selling and service work; professionals in public services; top structures in industry and commerce; and top structures in health services and local government. These topics do not represent any comprehensive or coherent list. Nor is the coverage of them even. Given our strong belief in problem-orientated work, and our consequent reliance on invitation, it could not be otherwise.[2] In some cases we have had the chance (as just indicated) to undertake work in particular settings in considerable depth over many years. In others, opportunities have been limited to a greater or lesser volume of shorter on-site projects, seminars or discussions – always supplemented, however, by a multiplicity of real-life case studies explored during the course of various Brunel-based workshops addressed to the particular topic in question.

What we have done in Part Two is simply to record (with due regard for confidentiality) whatever we have learned or gathered in whichever fields we have been able to work: sometimes much, sometimes little; sometimes in depth, sometimes more superficially. In each case we have attempted to present the findings in a way which helps to illustrate and fill out the general message of Part One. Nevertheless, particular readers may find certain chapters of Part Two of more interest than others.

Overall, then, we offer an approach to organisational design which, though it makes no claim to be all-encompassing, is nevertheless substantial both in its range of application and its depth of penetration. Above all it is an approach grounded (as much other writing on organisation is sadly not) on practical problems. It is built on decades of discussions with managers and practitioners from a wide variety of organisations on real and pressing problems as they actually manifest themselves. And it is dedicated to helping to bring such problems to practical resolution.

The tone of the approach itself has determined the way in which it has been written up in the pages which follow. We have aimed at two main groups of readership. The first are the many managers and other practitioners who desire to gain some deeper and more objective grasp of the complex organisational problems which regularly face them. The second are all those researchers, teachers and consultants who, though looking at the mainstream of organisational life from one remove, as it were, nevertheless retain a strong interest in practical as well as theoretical issues. With such readers in mind we have sought a style which is reasonably rigorous without being too 'academic'. As far as references to published work beyond that of ourselves and immediate colleagues is concerned, we have aimed at relevant points to note at least the main luminaries of the organisational literature of which the educated manager of today is likely to be aware.

Notes

1. The three main published accounts prior to this volume of the applications of work levels and other ideas described here to the area of public and voluntary services are to be found in E. Jaques, ed., *Health Services: Their Nature and Organisation, and the Role of Patients, Doctors, Nurses and the Complementary Professions*, London, Heinemann, 1978; D. Billis, G. Bromley, A. Hey and R. Rowbottom *Organising Social Services Departments*, London, Heinemann, 1980; and D. Billis, *Welfare Bureaucracies: Their Design and Change in Response to Social Problems*, London, Heinemann, 1984. Other publications in this area are mentioned in the notes on Chapters 9 and 11.

2. The particular methodology adopted for our work, with its strong emphasis on problem-orientation, is described in R. W. Rowbottom, *Social Analysis: A Colloborative Method of Gaining Usable Scientific Knowledge of Social Institutions*, London, Heinemann, 1977.

2   Clarifying Authority Relationships

In the previous chapter it was suggested that in large organisations many of the most obvious problems stem directly from unclear authority and responsibility. In this chapter this particular issue is examined in more detail. We start by considering the inadequacies of typical organisation charts in such matters and the way they regularly confuse *authority*, on the one hand, with *status, grade or pay level*, on the other. We go on to dispose of simplistic ideas like 'line and staff' and 'functional authority'. We discuss the true variety of relationship types, seven at least, which must be recognised if a proper basis is to be provided for effective organisational design in this area. We also note the frequent need to recognise and properly define not just one, but two *lines of authority* (thus giving the lie to equally over-simple ideas of 'unity of command'). Overall, we emphasise the importance of distinguishing pay or status hierarchies from management ones; and, within management hierarchies themselves, of distinguishing the key or main managerial roles from other authority-bearing roles of various kinds.

Typical Organisation Charts and their Shortcomings
When people start to describe in detail the problems and malfunctions of their own organisations they often produce as background to discussion some official chart. 'This', they say, 'is how we are organised at present'. But then invariably, they proceed to detail current realities of a kind which immediately throw the greatest doubts on the validity of the chart, or at least, on its reliability as a representation of how things actually occur in practice.

In commenting for example, on a factory organisation chart like that shown in Figure 2.1(a), they may perhaps observe that although the foremen are clearly shown as first-line managers they completely fail to live up to that image in practice; or that the superintendents regularly bypass the general foreman; or that although a works

Figure 2.1 Organisation charts as they are typically displayed

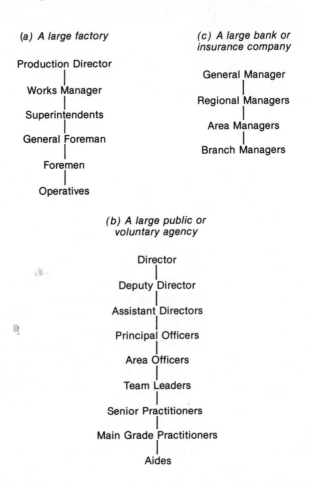

(a) *A large factory*

Production Director
|
Works Manager
|
Superintendents
|
General Foreman
|
Foremen
|
Operatives

(c) *A large bank or insurance company*

General Manager
|
Regional Managers
|
Area Managers
|
Branch Managers

(b) *A large public or voluntary agency*

Director
|
Deputy Director
|
Assistant Directors
|
Principal Officers
|
Area Officers
|
Team Leaders
|
Senior Practitioners
|
Main Grade Practitioners
|
Aides

manager post is prominently displayed, the production director has signally failed to delegate any significant authority or responsibility to its present incumbent. In discussions of the chart of some large public or voluntary agency like that shown in Figure 2.1(b), those involved may comment that the management role of team leaders is often very weak in relation to both senior and main-grade practitioners; that area officers do not regard themselves as in any way subordinate to principal officers; and that the authority of the deputy director is, to put it mildly, rather problematic. In describing the workings of some large bank or insurance company like that shown in Figure 2.1(c), those involved may immediately comment on the sizeable work overlap in practice between regional managers and area managers; or the very uncertain relation of superiority between the latter and heads of the larger or more important local branches. What, then, are typical organisation charts really about, and what are they really saying (at any rate as regards their vertical dimension)?

The first thing that they can usually be assumed to portray with reasonable accuracy is relative *status*: differences in pay and other material rewards and perquisites; differences in grades where grading systems are in use; differences in titular ranks in services (like police, fire, or nursing) where these are in use; differences in accompanying prestige. We should be surprised to find, for example, in the charts illustrated above, that general managers were paid less than regional managers; that area officers were on a lower grade than team leaders, or that the general foreman was regarded as of lower status than the ordinary foremen (although occasional anomalies might come to light, particularly in the form of overlapping pay scales).

The second thing we might suppose is that typical charts indicate something about relative *authority*: that all those in higher positions are able to give instructions of some kind to all those at the level below them. Here, however, assumptions might be regularly challenged by actual realities. It might very well be found (as suggested earlier) that in the factory example certain of the superintendents regarded themselves as totally outside the control of the works manager (in spite of being shown below the latter on chart) and liable to take instructions only from the production director. It might well be found in the public or voluntary agency concerned that no senior practitioner was in any position to give instructions to any main grade practitioner. It might be found in the bank or insurance company example that heads of larger branches completely rejected the authority of their so-called area managers.

Of course, the gap between official charts, so-called 'formal organisation', and actual realities, so-called 'informal organisation', is notorious. But what is not so often recognised is that informal organisation (if this term is to be employed) is usually by no means either obvious or simple itself. What is the 'real' structure is often a matter of doubt if not positive contention. And even where it is reasonably clear and accepted, it is invariably more complex than formal charts suggest.

It will usually be well known which levels in any given organisation are in fact the key managerial ones, the ones (regardless of particular occupants) which carry real responsibility and power. And there will often by a strong sense (even if it cannot be publicly voiced) of any managerial levels which are basically superfluous. But there will be many places where the jobs can be described in neither of these terms. There will be places where people are undertaking necessary work, but have in practice no authority whatsoever over those supposedly at the next level down, being more in the nature of senior colleagues carrying enhanced pay or grade for handling more difficult or complex projects. There will be places where people do have the right to allocate specific tasks on a daily basis to those at the next level down, but lack any longer-term responsibility for such things as career development, pay, or promotion. There will be jobs where people can convene meetings and issue instructions about detailed programmes, but cannot themselves initiate new projects or set new policies. There will be jobs where people have the right to check and report upon others' work, but cannot themselves change or redirect it if things are wrong. The very range of titles in use may hint at the many shades of difference in practice, more or less subtle: 'managers', 'supervisors', 'co-ordinators', 'chairmen', 'team leaders', 'seniors', 'controllers', 'inspectors', 'advisors', and so on.

Rarely, then, do all the vertical links on official charts stand for the same things in practice. Organisational life is more complex than typical organisational charts ever allow. A number of things have to be separated. Status, as marked by pay or grade, is one thing; whilst authority over others and responsibility for their work is another. And in this latter area, relationships can be of a variety of kinds.

Varieties of Authority Relationship
The fact that more than one kind of authority relationship is possible in typical large organisations does not of course always pass unrecognised. Dotted lines as well as full ones are sometimes added to official charts. A distinction is sometimes drawn between 'line' or 'managerial' authority on the one hand, and a second type variously described as 'functional', 'specialist', or 'professional' authority, on the other. But such a dual categorisation still does not go anything like far enough to catch the true variety of authority relationships which are actually to be found. Nor does it provide anything like fine enough instruments with which to resolve the sorts of practical problem which typically arise in this area. Does so-called 'functional' authority (or 'specialist' or 'professional' authority) include the right to appoint or dismiss staff? Does it include the right to reallocate resources or budgets? Does it include the right to prescribe new standards, assign new work programmes or set new policies? It is in respect of precisely such issues that the real contentions usually start to arise.

Explorations by ourselves and colleagues over many years have established the existence of at least *seven* different models of structured relationship in large organisations – see Table 2.1 – and there may well yet be others to be explicated.[1] (Although these models make reference to responsibilities as well as authority in relation to other people, it is the second element which is usually of prime concern; we may therefore refer to them briefly as 'authority relationships'.) The sense of these various models and the differences between them is most easily communicated by pointing to the different needs which each serves.

In all organisations of any significant size the common if not universal situation is this. On the one hand, the founding association and governing body between them define certain fundamental aims and objectives. On the other hand, there are the large number of individuals whose continuing work is necessary to bring these same aims and objectives to actuality. What is needed is the creation of a smaller number of key posts with full accountability for seeing that all the necessary work actually gets done, in the right order, by the right people, and in the right way. The occupants of these key posts will certainly not be able to do everything themselves. Their tasks essentially will be to get things done through other people. As such, it will usually be recognised that the holders of these key posts are not only responsible for the other people's work but (in some degree at least) for their general well-being and personal development.

Now, if there is to be such strong and comprehensive accountability there needs to be commensurate authority. It must logically include (in any ordinary employment situation) significant rights in the appointment of all subordinate staff, at minimum a veto. It must include rights to set general directions as well as specific tasks. It must include rights to make significant alterations in individual responsibilities according to how each performs in practice. It must include rights to record any formal appraisals of performance and capability, and rights at least to initiate, if not to directly execute, any changes in pay, regradings, transfers, or (in the extreme) dismissals. A job with this extensive degree of authority may be described as *main line-managerial*.

In the lower reaches of labour-intensive offices, factories, warehouses or the like, particularly those where staff turnover is high, a different sort of controlling post is often called for. There may already be a main line-manager (as just described) of commensurate status in overall charge. What such managers need are people to help with the onerous burden of inducting new staff, allocating numerous incoming jobs, dealing with minor stoppages or breakdowns, and

Table 2.1 Some common types of authority relationship

A *main line-managerial relationship* involves assigning duties and responsibility, appraising performance and ability, and forwarding staff development. It implies authority to join in selection of staff, to prescribe work in as much detail as may be required, and to initiate promotion, transfer or dismissal.

A *supervisory relationship* involves inducting, giving technical instruction, assigning tasks, checking performance, and helping with problems. Unlike a managerial relationship it does not imply authority to reallocate duties, or to initiate promotion, transfer or dismissal.

A *co-ordinating relationship* involves preparing and issuing detailed plans and programmes to forward agreed objectives, keeping informed of actual progress, and attempting to overcome obstacles and setbacks. It implies authority to obtain information of progress and to decide what shall be done in situations of uncertainty. It does not imply authority to set new directions, to override sustained disagreements, or to appraise personal performance or ability.

A *monitoring relationship* involves checking, or keeping informed of, the effect of others' activity in some given area; warning of sustained or significant deficiencies; and advising corrective action. It does not imply authority to give instruction or to appraise personal ability or performance.

A *collateral relationship* implies mutual dependence without any authority of one over the other. Sustained disagreements can ony be resolved by referral to some higher authority, where one exists.

A *service relationship* implies an obligation to respond to the stated needs of another, though in a manner and timing of choice.

A *prescribing relationship* implies the right to set specific tasks to be carried out, and the right to check results, but no other right to manage, supervise or direct.

---

providing continuous support and guidance. The people concerned will need to have authority to issue detailed job instructions and to check on performance. But the main line-manager will wish to retain the rights to make any major changes in responsibilities, or final judgements on personal capability, application or potential. Such auxiliary posts may be described as *supervisory*. (They also often arise, as discussed later, in the lower reaches of professional work.)

In other situations, yet another type of leadership role is often needed, one which carries neither main line-managerial authority nor that of a full-scale supervisor. Project leaders and committee chairmen often play such a role. So (knowingly or not) do many deputies and assistants. A certain stream of activities are to be progressed in a co-ordinated way and somebody is required to see that this happens. The person concerned needs rights to issue detailed plans and programmes, and rights to check on progress actually achieved, but no more. It is specifically required that such leaders do not take it upon themselves, unilaterally, to set new policies or to launch major initiatives. Such roles may be described as *co-ordinating*. Co-ordinating authority, unlike main line-managerial authority or supervisory authority, does not necessarily need to be backed by higher status or grade. Co-ordinators often act in relation to colleagues of just the same status level, sometimes on a temporary or rotating basis.

A fourth type of authority relationship springs from a need of quite a different kind, namely that of having one person who will concentrate on the maintenance of standards in some given area. Auditors and inspectors often play such a role. Such people require the right to check on what others are doing (in some defined respects), to discuss the situation with them, and to report to higher authorities on any sustained deficiencies. The individual involved might for example, be checking to see that safety regulations were being fully observed in practice; drawing attention to any breaches; discussing why in fact they were happening (perhaps out of simple carelessness or perhaps for good reason); deciding whether the breaches were important enough to report to a higher authority; and deciding whether, perhaps, to add some rider on the need to modify the regulations concerned. Such a role may be described as a *monitoring* one. The exercise of monitoring authority, like co-ordinating authority, does not call for any enhanced seniority or status. The two sorts of authority are often in fact combined in the same role, as for example in the jobs of specialist advisers of various kinds.

In work over the years in hospitals we have come across an authority relationship of yet another kind which is exemplified in the typical relationship of the doctor to the ward nurse. It is necessary for the former to be able to give instructions to the latter on specific work to be carried out on, or on behalf of, individual patients. However, all other elements of management are usually carried by more senior nursing staff. We have called such a relationship a *prescribing* one.

It is not always the case, of course, where two people work together, that the one needs to be (in common parlance) 'in authority' over the other. Indeed, there are many times when any attempt to create such a position would be artificial, if not positively inappropriate. The relationship between two colleagues whose work interacts, where neither has authority over the other, can be formally described as *collateral.* Common examples are the relationship of the production manager and sales manager both working on the same customers' orders, or two senior doctors collaborating on the same case, or two office managers sharing time on the same computer. A marked difference in level between collateral colleagues is rare, but it is by no means uncommon or impossible for one to have somewhat higher grade or pay than the other.

Finally, there is often the need to establish a situation where one person serves a number of others without being subordinate to any of them. This often arises in maintenance work, staff recruitment, or purchasing. The service-seeker will obviously need to be able to fix the basic requirements, but the service-giver will need authority to decide relative priorities and how in detail the work is best done. Such may be described as a *service* relationship. It differs from a collateral relationship in just this respect: in the service relationship one party decides the basic needs; in a collateral relationship both parties start from their own separate assessments.

It is worth checking at this point just how far these various definitions really do go beyond the old distinction of 'line' and 'staff'. Main line-managerial relationships, as just defined, certainly could be described more briefly as 'line' (provided again it was not assumed that every post shown 'in line' on the official chart carried in reality authority and responsibility of such a comprehensive kind). And the others, apart from the 'collateral' one, could at a stretch be described collectively as 'staff'. But the crucial point would have been missed. Main line-management posts are not simply to be taken as any that give instructions. And staff posts – if by this we mean the others – are certainly not be be characterised, as they so often are, as 'purely advisory'.

What is being pointed out here is that the reality of organisational life contains many different kinds of authority, not just the blanket right to 'give instructions'. Each particular type of authority makes its own characteristic impact. Setting general goals or policies for somebody – something associated only with main line-management posts as described here – is very different from the allocation of specific tasks. The first will be felt by those concerned to be a much more significant level of authority than the second. Most significant of all will be the right, or authority, to make formal appraisals of people's performance and capability, the right to change their responsibilities radically in consequence, and the right to affect their rewards, career, or continued employment. It is such authority, above all, that distinguishes the main line-management role from any other, not simply the 'authority to instruct'. It is the exercise of authority of just this sort that is what being a 'boss' is really about.

Dual Influence Situations

If all organisational authority is seen only in terms of possession or non-possession of a simple right to give instructions, then it would certainly appear wrong to let anybody be subject to two separate authority sources. This, in essence, is the principle of 'unity of command' – the idea that nobody can serve two masters. But once it is accepted that authority in organisation can be of many different kinds, the whole prospect changes. In fact no large modern organisation could possibly work if all instructions to any individual of whatever kind had to be channelled through one other person only. Any attempt to do so would immediately clog up the whole system. Typically, commands and instructions of different kinds have to come from a variety of different sources.

What often happens in practice is that an individual P (as shown in Table 2.2) finds in respect of some given area of work that he or she is subject to simultaneous influence or control from two distinct figures, A and B. A could in a particular case be, for example, the official line-manager of P, and B some senior specialist or adviser, assistant or deputy, who is also in regular contact. In another situation, A could be the chief of the local office or factory in which P works, and B a headquarters manager in the same specialist field as P (finance, say, or personnel work). In another instance again, A could be head of a special project group of which P is a member and B his or her permanent divisional head. In the circumstance where P is a member of some multi-disciplinary team of professional practitioners, A could be the leader of the team concerned and B a senior officer in the same profession as P, located outside the team. (Many of these and similar cases are explored in more detail in later chapters.)

In all such 'dual-influence' situations (as they may be called) there is without doubt a powerful potential for conflict and confusion. But the answer is rarely, if ever, to deny the basic reality of the situation, to try and do away completely with one or other of the two lines of influence. It is to grapple positively with the problem, and decide the optimum division of authority between the two lines.

In doing this, it may sometimes become rapidly evident that one of the lines is (in the terms introduced in the last section) best regarded as main line-managerial and the other as perhaps co-ordinating, or monitoring, or supervisory, or prescribing (or some combination of these). On other occasions, however, it may not be so easy to describe the appropriate model in any of these precise terms. In this case it is necessary to look in detail at the various aspects of P's situation or activity shown in the check-list in Table 2.2, and decide in relation to each, the best allocation of authority as between A and B: who should appoint P, induct and train P, appraise P's performance, set methods and standards for P, and so on. On certain items, authority and responsibility may be seen to rest with one party only. On others, it may feel appropriate for both parties to be jointly involved, whether or not it is up to one of them to take the prime initiative. Sometimes, indeed, it may become apparent that the necessary sharing of key decisions about P is such that the outcome can only be described as one of 'co-management'. (In this last case, any higher post or body with 'cross-over' authority which exists, will serve an important function in dealing with unresolved disputes between A and B about the conduct of P and P's work.[2])

Table 2.2 Dual influence situations: a check-list

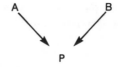

How is authority to be exercised, or shared, as between A and B, in respect of P's:

- appointment?
- induction and training?
- performance appraisal?
- pay and grading?
- dismissal, suspension or transfer?
- responsibilities and organisation?
- methods and standards?
- policies and programmes?
- resources and budgets?

Achieving Clearer Authority Relationships
Uncertainties about authority and responsibility, then, are common-place in large organisations. Typically, they are left unresolved by official charts which commonly fail to distinguish authority from grade, pay or status and, in any case, usually make allowance for only one type of relationship. Nor are attempts to define relationships in broad terms like 'line', 'staff', 'functional' or 'professional' usually any better. Much more detailed definition is needed. And the regular possibility of two (or more) lines of authority has to be accepted.

However, there are problems and problems about authority. The most acute in our experience are undoubtedly those that spring from uncertainties about key managerial roles – main line-managerial roles, as we have now defined them. Organisations are very prone to try and create, or to assume unthinkingly, the existence of far too many levels of main managerial roles. Over-obsession with spans of control frequently causes extra levels to be built in (a problem to be explored more thoroughly in later pages). It is not uncommon for additional management posts to be created simply to accommodate senior people who would otherwise be redundant. And last but not least, where grading systems exist, there are frequently strong pressures to ensure that each and every grade is represented by its own separate level in the management hierarchy.

The results of any such proliferation of management levels, or apparent management levels, are all too predictable. There is pervasive uncertainty about who should really be taking action on current problems. Things are constantly having to be 'referred up' for ratification. Bypassing becomes endemic. Resentment grows against supposed bosses who do not seem capable of grasping their proper responsibilities. Corresponding resentment follows against supposed subordinates who do not offer appropriate support and loyalty. How many so-called 'personality clashes' have roots in just such structural anomalies!

The first step in any systematic design or redesign approach to this area is to bring out clearly which of any existing or proposed posts really are to be main line-management ones. The second is to define the exact authority, if any, to be exercised by all others in the status chain. (We will assume for the moment that all existing or proposed posts are needed; under what circumstances this is likely to be untrue can be better discussed after work-level ideas have been introduced in the next chapter.)

Thus, returning to the factory example discussed earlier such an exercise might possibly confirm (Figure 2.2(a)) that both the production director and superintendents occupied, at different levels, posts of a main line-managerial kind, but that the so-called works manager might better be conceived as a general assistant to the production director, exercising co-ordinating authority (as just defined). It might suggest that some of the foremen, the more senior, were in a position to play main line-managerial roles, but that other more junior ones might be better recognised as carrying only super-visory authority (as just defined).

In the public or voluntary agency example discussed, analysis of this sort might suggest in a particular case (Figure 2.2(b)) that the director, assistant directors, and area officers were the ones (at their various levels) who operated most closely to the main line-management model, whilst the deputy and principal officers were better seen as in co-ordinating and monitoring roles of some kind. It might suggest that team leaders had two distinct roles to play, one main line-managerial in relation to aides, the other monitoring and co-ordinating in relation to fellow-practitioners.

In the banking or insurance example discussed, it might suggest (Figure 2.2.(c)) that area managers would be in a position to exercise main line-managerial authority in relation to heads of smaller branches, but only co-ordinating or monitoring authority in relation to heads of larger ones. (Figure 2.2 shows more fully-explicated charts, although we do not suggest that charting alone can ever provide the detail necessary for adequate specification.)

It must be stressed that any such exercise is not simply one of detailed portrayal of existing realities as they stand but, to a greater or lesser degree, a redesign or remodelling of them. It is not simply one of academic description, but of clarification and change. Existing realities certainly need careful study to get a sense of what is really going on; which roles are strong and which weak; what is working well and what is not. But the whole point is to produce specifications which overcome existing or potential difficulties, which solve problems. And indeed, any act of precise description becomes in itself part of the change. Where, for example, posts generally regarded as 'strong' are more formally announced as possessing the full range of authority detailed in the main line-managerial description above, something significant has happened. People might up to this point have had a vague perception of how things stood, but an explicit, detailed statement is different. Even if there is in any given setting a general consensus on who is the 'boss' (itself a by no means predictable situation), this does not imply that all necessarily understand, let alone agree, on exactly what this means in terms of acceptable action and powers. The potential benefits from a careful specification of posts currently experienced as weak are even more obvious.

Figure 2.2 Organisation charts with explication of different authority relationships

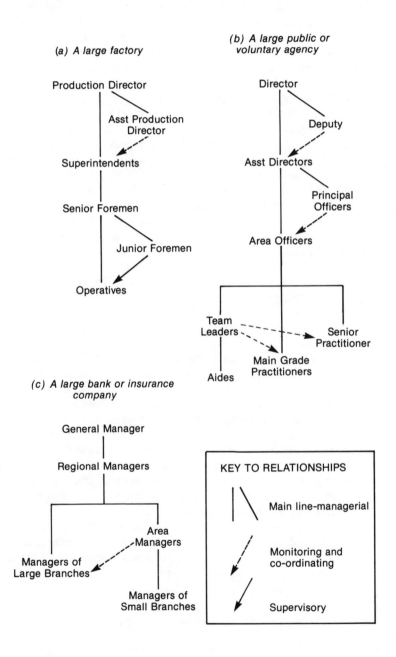

(a) A large factory

Production Director

Asst Production Director

Superintendents

Senior Foremen

Junior Foremen

Operatives

(b) A large public or voluntary agency

Director

Deputy

Asst Directors

Principal Officers

Area Officers

Team Leaders

Senior Practitioner

Main Grade Practitioners

Aides

(c) A large bank or insurance company

General Manager

Regional Managers

Area Managers

Managers of Large Branches

Managers of Small Branches

KEY TO RELATIONSHIPS

Main line-managerial

Monitoring and co-ordinating

Supervisory

Conclusion

To sum up, the hierarchies shown on conventional organisational charts are apt to give a grossly misleading and oversimplified view of realities. They may often provide a reasonably accurate picture of relative status as measured by things like pay, grade, rank or perquisites, but cannot be relied upon to give any adequate indication of relative authority and responsibility. Part of the problem is the paucity of terms for describing these latter dimensions. Crude notions of 'line and staff', 'functional authority', and the like, can never hope to catch the variety of relationships called for in reality in large complex organisations. Detailed studies over the years have revealed at least seven different relationships, all reasonably commonplace, which have to be distinguished – main line-managerial, supervisory, co-ordinating, monitoring, prescribing, collateral and service. The identification and definition of such conceptions is a big step forward in organisational design. It allows many problems of confusion or conflict in relationships in existing organisations to be settled with certainty. And it reduces the incidence of such problems when new organisations are brought into being.

The conception of a main line-management role whose occupant has authority not just to give detailed working instructions but to appraise suitability for particular jobs and to affect rewards and future activities accordingly, allows a decisive separation of management structures from hierarchies of status or grading. Clearer definitions can be provided for management posts already felt to be 'strong', alternative possibilities can be examined for others generally felt to be 'weak'.

Yet such analysis, good as far as it goes, leaves many important issues still unaddressed. Individuals apart, what in general causes this phenomenon of 'strong' and 'weak' levels? Exactly how many 'strong', that is, 'main line-management', levels is it possible to establish? Does this vary with size of organisation? How does the actual task in main line-management posts vary from level to level, from first level to middle level, and from middle level to top level? Do these terms, first, middle and top, stand for the same kind of work in all organisations, big or small? Is it possible to have a situation where front-line, non-managerial workers in one organisation are doing work of the same level or responsibility as that undertaken by main line-managers in another organisation (or is all 'management' work automatically higher than 'non-management' work, however responsible)? It is to these further questions that we now turn.

Notes

1.   For further details and discussion of these various authority relationships see R.W.

Rowbottom, A.M. Hey and D. Billis, *Social Services Departments: Developing Patterns of Work and Organisation*, London, Heinemann, 1974, Appendix A, and E. Jaques, *A General Theory of Bureaucracy*, London, Heinemann, 1976, Chapters 4 and 17. (It will be noted that we have now adopted the term 'main line-managerial' rather than the softer and broader term 'managerial', to stand for the first relationship described in the text, in order to minimise possible confusion or ambiguity). Most other writers go no further than a dual categorisation: 'line' versus 'staff'; 'administrative' versus 'professional'; 'structural' versus 'sapiential', and so on. Jay Galbraith is an exception in noting the practical need to distinguish at any rate four different degrees of authority in any decision process: (in shorthand form) 'responsible', 'approve', 'consult', 'inform'. See J. Galbraith, *Designing Complex Organisations*, Reading, MA, Addison-Wesley, 1973.

2. For further discussion of 'dual influence' situations see Rowbottom *et al. Social Services Departments*; Jaques, *Bureaucracy*; also K. Knight, *Matrix Management*, Farnborough, Gower Press, 1977.

3　Distinguishing Work Levels

The clearer identification of various types of authority relationship can be a great help in dealing with many organisational problems, but leaves (as noted at the end of the last chapter) many deeper questions about managerial and operational structures still unanswered.

We come now to describe a theory of work levels which was developed in response to such questions: to things like what in general causes 'strong' and 'weak' layers of management; how the essential nature of managerial work differs at bottom, middle and top levels; how high-responsibility jobs without managerial functions relate to managerial ones, and so on. In this chapter we describe the theory in detail, and discuss its prime application, namely, the provision of a precise guide to the optimum number of management levels in a given organisation of any given size or scope; a guide to where weak levels will emerge if this number is exceeded, and where the chain will be felt to be incomplete if levels are missed out.

Describing Work Levels
The consciousness that work in organisation varies in level as well as in kind is widespread. Frequent contrasts are made in common parlance for example between 'top' jobs and 'run of the mill' jobs; between 'responsible' jobs and 'routine' ones. Such vague terms are no great use in organisational design, however. Nor do they help resolve contentious problems. The senior hospital doctor and its head porter, for example, can both be said to be carrying out 'responsible' work. The director of the small building firm and the director of the multi-national company may both be described as in 'top' jobs.

Various writers – Lyndall Urwick, T. T. Patterson and Stafford Beer, for example – have attempted more-systematic descriptions. But most of these fail, in our view, to provide categories of any precision or conceptual weight. They tend to be biased to one particular type of role, 'managerial' (and very often to managerial roles in industry).

And, like colloquial usage, they typically fail to cope with the factor of absolute size, to distinguish large enterprises from small ones.[1]

Elliott Jaques was the first person to develop a general theory of work levels of real substance and applicability. His particular image is described primarily in terms of the varying time dimension in work, and in the qualitative differences in mental ability needed to tackle work of different time-scales.[2] However, time measures are not, in our experience, easy ones to use in detailed organisational design or problem-solving. And the theory offers no very clear picture of the actual quality of output or end-product required in work and how it varies from level to level. (Nevertheless, his ideas have been very influential on our own thinking, and the two sets of ideas, his and ours, are complementary rather than opposing.)

Our own ideas on work levels originated from research and consultancy in large social welfare organisations.[3] As the ideas developed we were able to test them extensively in health services and voluntary organisations, and in various discussions and projects with people from other public services, commerce and industry.

Gradually, the following picture emerged. Regardless of the particular field – social work, nursing, engineering, banking or whatever – all organised work, managerial or non-managerial, falls into a hierarchy of discrete levels or strata, in which the range of the objectives to be achieved, on the one hand, and the range of environmental circumstances to be taken into account, on the other, broaden and change in quality at successive steps. Each step upwards demands an ever deeper and more comprehensive response to the world and its various needs and possibilities. Work at successively higher strata will always be experienced as more responsible, though significant, if finer differences of responsibility are possible within any given strata – in other words, there are sub-levels within levels. The main levels form a natural framework for delegation and control, and hence provide, amongst other things, the basis for an optimum structure of management.

The first five levels or strata (we will use the first and simpler term from now on) may be described in brief as, *prescribed output, situational response, systematic provision, comprehensive provision* and *field coverage*. These five levels cover the expected work in even the largest operating units, individual service agencies, or manufacturing companies. But higher levels also exist. At least two can be identified – *multi-field coverage* and *meta-field coverage*. Typically these arise at the top of major corporations, Departments of State, or large local authorities.

It should be stressed from the beginning that these various levels are absolute, not relative. Not every organisation spans all five (or seven) levels. (On the contrary, work levels provide a scale by which the size of various organisations can be precisely indicated; one which is more fundamental than either numbers of staff, financial turnover, or asset value.)

The different work levels may now be described in more detail, starting with the first five (overviewed in Table 3.1), then proceeding to two possible higher ones (overviewed in Table 3.2).

Table 3.1 Summary of first five work levels

Work level	Title	Expected work
5	*Field coverage*	Covering a general field of need throughout a society.
4	*Comprehensive provision*	Providing a complete range of products or services throughout a whole territorial or organisational society.
3	*Systematic provision*	Making systematic provision according to the needs of a flow of open-ended situations.
2	*Situational response*	Carrying out concrete tasks whose precise objectives have to be judged according to each situation encountered.
1	*Prescribed output*	Carrying out concrete tasks whose objectives are completely specifiable beforehand as far as is significant.

Level 1: Prescribed Output

At the first level, work consists of a number of separate, concrete, tasks each of whose end-products is completely prescribed or prescribable (see Figure 3.1).

There is some pre-designed object to be made, some given service to be rendered, some specific information to be collected, some prescribed test or check to be carried out. What is to be done, in terms of the kind or form of results to be achieved, does not have to be decided. It will either have been specifically prescribed for the occasion, or communicated during induction or training as the sort of response required whenever a certain kind of situation arises. If there is any doubt on the subject it can be dispelled by further description or demonstration to the point where more detailed discrimination becomes irrelevant to the quality of result required. And if there is any doubt about whether to pursue the task in the first place, the matter can be referred to a superior. In effect, all legitimate demands are to be met without further query or ado.

Figure 3.1

Examples of level 1 work are such things as typing a letter from manuscript or tape, checking an invoice, making a piece of furniture to a set specification, repairing a piece of faulty equipment, cleaning a room, undertaking a routine test, or carrying out a set procedure for reception of visitors.

It should be stressed that it is the prescription of output or end-product only that characterises level 1 work. How much else is prescribed will vary, but there will always be something left to the discretion of the worker concerned. Even at this level, the work is not totally 'programmed'.[4] There will usually be scope for some choice of method. Judgement will also be called for where, for example, raw materials of variable character or quality are to be processed (as in much production work), or where the peculiarities of human nature are to be tactfully dealt with (as in much services work). Work at the bottom of level 1, so-called unskilled work, may leave very little room for individual discretion. (In the extreme, where virtually all discretion has been deliberately removed from a job, there is a prime case for automation of some kind – in other words, we are no longer talking of human work.) However, work at the top of level 1, the realm of the craftsman, the senior clerk, and the working supervisor, may often demand considerable judgement and experience.

Level 2: Situational Response

At the second level, work still consists essentially of dealing one by one with concrete situations or problems as they arise. But now there is a significant change. Now the precise response to each situation has to be left to the judgement of the worker concerned (see Figure 3.2). Demands can now no longer be taken at their face value; there is always an implicit requirement to explore and find out what the 'real' needs are. What is to be done can be settled only in broad terms beforehand. Until the task is actually tackled, only a general indication of the optimum outcome can be given.

Figure 3.2

Level 2 work often involves making an assessment of, and then attending to, the needs of other people – clients, employees, students, patients, and so on. Whereas at level 1 it is for the most part a question of giving the customer what he asks for, at level 2 it is always a case of finding out what he really wants or needs. The typical level 1 task of gathering specific information is transformed at level 2 into that of producing a rounded appraisal or report. Typing letters changes to composing them. Giving instruction to a set form (as in much basic training) changes to the provision of some kind of genuine education. Providing pills on demand (as in retail pharmacy) becomes supplying diagnosis-based treatment (as in medical practice). And so on.

At level 2, the first *main line-managerial* posts emerge, that is, those which carry full accountability for the work of level 1 workers and the task of assessing their needs and capabilities, allocating duties accordingly and promoting personal development. (In contrast, *supervisory* roles, as detailed in Chapter 2, may exist in the upper reaches of level 1, but those in them will not be excepted to make rounded appraisals of the ability and needs of subordinate staff, but rather to carry out such prescribed tasks as instructing newcomers in their work, allocating specific tasks and dealing with specific queries.) However, it is not necessary to assume that all roles within level 2 have a managerial content. Indeed, the kind of definitions proposed here and below surmount the problem of being forced to describe higher-than-basic levels of work in a way which automatically links them to the carrying of managerial or supervisory responsibility. As we shall see later, many professional staff like engineers, teachers and social workers are in jobs with a level 2 work expectation even though they do not control or manage any subordinates.

Level 3: Systematic Provision

At level 3 the basic requirement changes again. It is no longer sufficient to deal with situations on a one-by-one basis, however excellently. Now a continuous sequence of concrete needs must be encompassed, including those yet to come as well as those already in hand (see Figure 3.3). Within given staffing and physical facilities, and some framework of the general *kind* of product or service to be provided, the essential job is to develop a systematic response to the flow of changing needs as a whole. This means not only dealing with the needs of today but constantly developing the system by which the needs of tomorrow are to be met. Inevitably, some degree of concept-ualisation is involved. Although the kind of product or service to be provided is given, there is much scope for technical improvement and innovation, for thinking of new ways of organising and utilising given people, buildings and equipment to produce better, more copious, or cheaper results.

Figure 3.3

Typical examples of level 3 work are such things as developing and introducing a better procedure for dealing with clients, customers or patients, or a better system for handling orders or complaints, or an improved negotiating procedure in industrial relations, or a new educational curriculum.

Of course, there can also be work at level 2 which involves the specification of systems, rules or procedures. But at that lower level any such work will (by definition) be setting a framework for prescribed-output activity. At level 3 the systems concerned are themselves designed to encompass genuine open-ended cases. As well as firm prescriptions, there will therefore be many general directional guides: 'give special attention to first-time customers', 'give first priority to child-abuse cases', 'tighten up on staff discipline', 'devote more attention to complaints' and so on. At level 3, then, the first genuine policy-making arises.

Level 4: Comprehensive Provision
At level 4 the definition of the aims to be achieved and the environmental situation to be encompassed again take a clear jump. No longer is it sufficient just to continue to produce a flow of services of existing kinds in response to needs as they spontaneously arise, however systematically or efficiently. Further initiative is required. An output must be engineered which is comprehensive both in terms of range and in terms of coverge of some given territorial or organisational society (see Figure 3.4). If there are significant gaps in either respect, they must be attended to. Both the introduction of new products or services and the withdrawal of old ones must be constantly considered. Needs across the whole of the social territory must be taken account of regardless of whether they are yet actually manifest, and regardless of whether the necessary facilities to respond to them are yet in being. If necessary, market research or other systematic surveys must be mounted in order to discover the full extent of potential need. Overall, a strong sense of balance and priorities is called for.

Figure 3.4

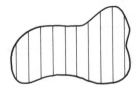

At level 3, work always has to be done within given concrete resources – the actual people available, the particular equipment and facilities which exist. Actual cash expenditure must be managed within given limits. Specific bids can be submitted for additional resources. But this is as far as it goes. At level 4 a broader overview is necessary. The complete range must be surveyed, comprehensive plans produced, and comprehensive budgets negotiated. The whole picture will often need to be translated into financial terms so that the net effects of changes in various parts can be readily seen. Investment in new plant and buildings, and major recruitment and training programmes, must frequently be considered, even if higher approval is needed before action can proceed.

As regards this last point, since capital expenditure is always a sensitive issue, as (particularly in public services) are the size and divisions of the major budget allocation, final sanction for these things will rest with governing boards or committees. (Consequently, work at level 4 involves keeping in close touch with the governing process: in commercial companies, indeed, executives at this level will frequently be given board appointments.) Those working at level 4 will not themselves have authority to incur major investment expenditure, or to make large-scale changes in any other budgets (even though they must produce well thought through proposals), but they will nevertheless typically possess the right to make some limited reallocation of resources. In industry they will usually have rights to incur minor capital expenditure up to predetermined limits. In public services they will usually have rights to exercise virement (the shifting of resources from one budget head to another to balance overspends and underspends), again, up to some given limit.

An example of level 4 work in industry is that of providing a major manufacturing facility, the buildings, the equipment and the people, able to produce the whole range of product lines likely to be required for sale in some given territorial market or markets. In the nursing field (to take a different case) a typical level 4 job is to develop and maintain a comprehensive nursing organisation for a large general hospital covering all the established branches of ward and out-patient work – general surgical, medical, paediatric, theatre and intensive care, and so on.

Level 5: Field Coverage

At Level 5, the whole of some territorial or organisational society has again to be considered, but the scope is broadened by moving from a framework of some given or established range of products or services to one which merely specifies some general field of need. The task is to produce an output which covers the whole field in relation to the whole of the given society as well as possible (see Figure 3.5). This means developing complete new ranges of products or services, or dropping existing ranges now ineffective or out of date. Such changes must be rooted not only in what is desirable, but what is socially, politically and financially possible. The work involves not just the production of concrete plans, but long-term strategies. It involves not just the fixing of detailed budgets but broader financial management – the assessment of long-term economic and commerical trends, the negotiation or procurement of new capital or revenue, the handling of reserve funds, and so on.

Figure 3.5

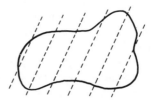

Within industry a move from level 4 to level 5 will be marked by a much more open definition of the product field. At level 4 terms like 'kitchen chairs', 'microscopes' or 'telephones' may be used. At level 5 broader terms like 'furniture', 'scientific instruments' or 'communications equipment' become more appropriate. In the health-care field the aim will shift from delivering conventional surgical, medical or midwifery facilities to, more simply, providing a 'health service'. In the welfare field it will change from things like the provision of standard case-work services or residential homes, to dealing as best as possible with all social breakdown. And so on.

In general, a level 4 definition will always allow a concrete image of the product or service to be conjured up – and in consequence a precise picture of the sorts of physical facilities and staff needed to provide it. A level 5 definition will allow no such precise interpretation; within the broad field-description, all will be possible, all will be open.

Higher Work Levels
So far we have described five distinct levels of work. We have tested these particular descriptions with many thousands of managers and others and found, by and large, that they stand up well. Taken together, they account for the complete range of work to be found in even quite large industrial companies and public agencies. But there are undoubtedly higher levels still, although exactly how many is uncertain. At this point we ourselves can only offer specific descriptions of two further levels beyond the five just described (thus

making seven in total). Even these must be considered as tentative and provisional formulations. We recognise that the descriptions are, at this point, rather abstract and difficult. (However, the sense of what we are driving at may come over rather more strongly when particular applications are described in Part Two.)

Table 3.2 Summary of higher work levels

Work level	Title	Expected work
7	*Meta-field coverage*	Covering a meta-field of need throughout a society.
6	*Multi-field coverage*	Covering a given complex of fields of need throughout a society.

Level 6: Multi-Field Coverage
The next step beyond level 5 seems to be about covering not just one, but a whole complex of fields of need, a complex whose constituent parts are all pre-given. The task is to ensure that an output is produced which covers all the given fields in a coordinated way, in relation to the whole of the given society.

There are in fact two main possibilities. In one a number of different fields of need are to be covered simultaneously in relation to the same or much the same territory. One example might be the work falling on the chief executive of a commercial group consisting of several large operating companies, including, say, a leisure-services firm, a large travel agency, a hotel chain, and a catering company, all covering broadly the same ground. Another example might be the work of the chief executive of a large local authority, whose job it is to bring together the activities of a number of major services like education, social welfare, police, housing, planning, and works, for the locality concerned. A third example might be the job of the dean of a sizeable university faculty consisting of a cluster of related academic departments like physics, metallurgy, chemistry, and biology.

Another possibility is that similar fields of need are to be covered simultaneously in several different territories each with its own level 5 operating unit. One example here might be the work falling on a chief executive of a group making or marketing the same type of product in distinct level 5 operating units in several neighbouring European countries, say. Another might be that of a British Regional Health Authority coordinating the work of up to a dozen separate District Health Authorities, each themselves working to a level 5 brief.

Whatever the case, at level 6 the task is not only to ensure effective coverage of each of the separate fields, but to see that the whole develops as a unified system. In effect, there is a conglomerate of level 5 operating units to be managed (*conglomerate management* might be another way of characterising work at this level). Key work includes formulating integrated strategies and programmes, setting the main cross-field priorities, settling differential allocations of resources, determining any necessary revision in internal boundaries, and handling any conflicts between the constituent parts.

At this level there is no systematic consideration of how the profile of the complex might extend or change. Level 5 units are added or lost in an *ad hoc* fashion, or on specific instruction from higher levels. However, it is crucial that the complex or conglomerate does form some recognisable entity in its own right, that the constituent level 5 units do in fact interact.

Level 7: Meta-Field Coverage
There appears to be a level above level 6 which does include responsibility for a more systematic development of level 5 operating units. It may be that chief executives of groups of commercial companies, the very top officers of central governmental departments, and vice-chancellors of universities are expected to operate at this higher level.

Level 7 work seems to be about operating in fields which are of a nature and size which require the creation of various complexes or conglomerates of level 5 units (each of the latter with their own defined sub-fields), if significant impact or coverage is to be achieved. The overall task is to ensure that an output is produced which covers the whole of the meta-field in relation to the whole of the given society. A key activity is systematic scanning within the meta-field concerned to see where new level 5 units are required or old ones no longer required, and changing the pattern and content of level 6 complexes accordingly.

What, then, it may be asked, is the difference between a 'general field of need' (level 5 or 6) and a 'meta-field' (level 7)? The example of State health care in Britain may furnish a possible answer. The job of the current District Health Authorities is arguably to cover the comprehensive needs for health *services* (as such) in their particular districts, but no more. By contrast, the job of the Central Health Authority – the Secretary of State for Health and his staff – is arguably to cover the meta-field of *health* itself (that is, not merely health services). Delivering health services may mean many and diverse things, but clearly excludes, for example, the provision of housing or general education. On the other hand, a systematic response to the meta-field of health as a whole, may well involve interventions in both these latter areas: sponsoring certain building regulations in housing, say, or programmes of health education in schools. In the field of health care, then, 'health' (in the broadest sense) describes the meta-field, and dealing with this is level 7 work. 'Health services' describes one subsidiary part, and dealing with this is level 5 work. (In this particular case, as just suggested, the level 6 work is probably handled by the Regional Health Authorities).

In other areas the move from level 5 to level 7 may be marked by changes in terminology such as 'furniture' to 'domestic products', 'scientific instruments' to 'engineering', 'communication equipment' to 'electronics' – a further step in abstraction. Whereas at level 5 (and level 6) there is still a clear idea of responding to the needs of specific markets or sections of the population, this quite disappears at level 7. At level 5 one can hope to identify what particular sorts of people or businesses in any given population at any given time are likely to need, for example, furniture, scientific instruments or communication equipment. But anybody and everybody may need domestic products, engineering products and (nowadays) electronic equipment. And anybody and everybody is concerned about health, education, housing, employment, defence and the like – for which reason no doubt it is in just such general terms that the responsibilities of ministers in national governments are described.[5]

The Status of the Ideas
We have now described seven separate work levels. What, it may be asked, is the hard evidence for the existence of these levels? This is not a straightforward question to answer. It cannot be simply a matter of going out and collecting data about existing jobs which proves that they all fall naturally into one or other of these five or more slots. On the contrary, it is often quite difficult to decide which of the levels any given job equates with. But this is not because the schema is lacking in some way. It is because, as already noted, there is often – very often indeed – confusion in the minds of the people concerned about exactly what *is* expected in a given job. Is a typical staff nurse in a hospital ward expected to make open-ended appreciation of ward problems (level 2), or merely to carry-out a complex series of prescribed tasks, referring to higher levels wherever unsure (level 1)? Is a particular factory manager expected to provide a comprehensive production

facility for the coming years (level 4) or, more simply, to develop systematic production methods and programmes within a set of capital and human resources decided by higher management (level 3)? In such cases, a work-level analysis does not simply portray evident facts, but offers ways of responding to real confusions or uncertainties.

The work-level schema is not, then, just a simple picture or description of how the world is, any more than the various definitions of authority relationships set out in the previous chapter. All are best thought of as *models*. They are models which have grown out of the experience of a wide range of different work settings and enterprises, and are thus firmly rooted in reality. But at the end of the day, they are ones which suggest how things could be or should be shaped (particularly, as we say, when there is uncertainty or confusion): ways not just of classifying things, but of clarifying them. We would certainly hope that the reader finds some reflection of realities as he or she already knows them in these ideas. But in the end, the test is not conformity to purported facts, *but one of practical usefulness*. For us, as for the practising administrator or organisational designer, the ultimate questions must be: do these ideas throw new light on practical problems? Which particular ones do they illuminate? What do they lead to by way of concrete options or guidance?

Aligning Work Levels and Main Management Levels

The first practical issue on which work-level ideas throw new light is that of the optimum number of levels in management structures. As noted in the previous chapter, uncertainties about where the main levels really are in such structures can lead to duplication, bypassing, and all sorts of attendant confusions and anxieties. The first necessary step, as we have seen, is to sort out of just what a main line-management role means and to distinguish it from other roles of lesser authority and responsibility. But this alone is not enough. Even a structure in which all main line-management roles are clearly indicated, spelt out and separated from the rest, may still have too many levels, or too few. The work-level analysis allows another essential requirement to be formulated. The basic proposition is as follows: *the optimum management structure has one but only one main line-management post in each successive work-level above the first*. (It may be noted again that no main line-management post can exist at level 1, since the activity involved requires at least a 'situational response' outlook; although supervisory posts of some kind are possible.)

The general reasons for this are pretty evident. Suppose it is attempted to introduce a main line-management post at some point in an organisation as in Figure 3.6, such that its occupant B is doing work of essentially the same level as his so-called subordinate C, albeit perhaps handling tasks of greater complexity and responsibility. What happens when C wants, from time to time, as he surely must, guidance and help on some problem or series of problems which he is finding difficulty in tackling?

Figure 3.6

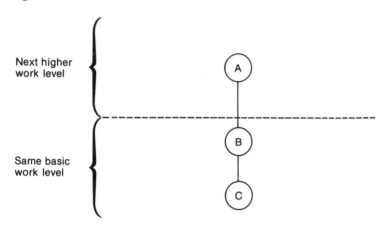

What C will discover is that, although B may be willing and able to give help and advice up to a point, beyond that he is forced to say, 'we had better both go and discuss this with A, since I cannot see any good way out of this myself, or since I can go no further within the scope of my own job and authority'. Over time, C will come to perceive B not as an authoritative manager is his own right, but as at best a respected senior colleague and at worst a positive nuisance. Almost certainly C will get into the habit of making direct approaches to A himself when the issues are weighty enough.

In fact what people want from a real boss or manager (as compared to an immediate supervisor, adviser, coordinator, or senior colleague in the role of monitor) is somebody who, if the difficulties and problems seem significant enough, can help by altering the basic context of their work. They want a boss who is able by virtue of his or her position (assuming abilities to match) to see the world with a qualitatively different perspective. They want one who can, where necessary, alter the whole system in some way; operate a different set of signals and levers; make available new types of resource; initiate new trains of investigation or negotiation. They want one who is in a position to overview the whole field of their activity, provide them with some authoritative assessment of their performance from a higher standpoint; set them going in quite new directions; head them off from others. In short, they want a boss whose own job is based in work at the next level up to that of their own.

As noted in Chapter 2, there appears a strong tendency for many organisations, obsessed with innumerable minor differences in status or grade, to try to operate with too many levels of management – with the results also noted. Occasionally, however, the opposite happens: they try to act with too *few* levels of management, as illustrated in Figure 3.7. The results are almost as bad. Unless B happens in effect to be much too good for his job, he will be incapable of working at the next work level up. A himself will therefore have to try and cover work at two distinct levels – with the likelihood that neither is done well. A will usually fail to give to B the necessary level of support and guidance. B will often fail to refer issues up the line which should be so referred, simply because his boss is (in his eyes) such a remote, Olympian, being.

Figure 3.7

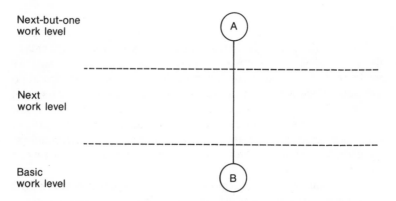

Deciding Optimum Numbers of Main Management Levels

From what has been said it follows that, once in any given organisation there is clear understanding about the highest and lowest work levels to be undertaken (two other basic design issues to which we will return in due course), then there is a definite answer to the optimum number of management levels required, irrespective of the

Figure 3.8 Organisation charts with explication of different authority relationships and explication of expected work levels

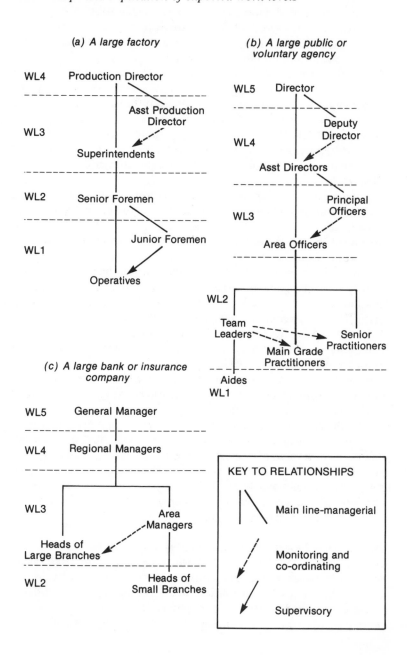

business or activity concerned.

Thus to consider further the examples raised in Chapter 2, if the factory concerned (Figure 3.8(a)) was reasonably large, it might well be agreed that the production director was expected to operate at level 4 in developing and maintaining a comprehensive set of production facilities. Assuming that shop-floor operatives worked at level 1, then there would be room for two intermediate main management levels as shown. If the factory concerned was much smaller, however, then it might be that a more realistic brief for the so-called production director would be to maintain and develop a given set of productive facilities (level 3), the level 4 work being done elsewhere. In this case either the superintendent level or the senior foreman level would be redundant as main line-management ones (for further discussion, see Chapter 7).

If the public or voluntary agency concerned (Figure 3.8(b)) was a very large one it might well be that the expectation of the top post was to cover some complete field of need like housing or welfare, that is to operate at level 5. If the main-grade practitioners were professionals, they would probably be expected to work at level 2, with help from various aides at level 1. In this case there would be room again for exactly two main line-management levels in between, perhaps for assistant directors with a level 4 brief, and area officers with a level 3 brief. However, were the organisation smaller, with a top post at level 4 instead of level 5, there would only be room for one intermediate management level between this and the front-line professionals at level 2 (for further discussion see Chapters 9 and 11).

If the bank or insurance company concerned (Figure 3.8(c)) was large enough, its general manager might also be expected to operate at level 5. Heads of larger branches might well be expected to operate at level 3, heads of smaller ones at level 2. If regional managers carried level 4 responsibilities there would be room for one further management level in respect of smaller branches but not larger ones. Hence any area managers at level 3 might be required to carry a mixed role: main line-managerial in respect of some branch heads, monitoring and co-ordinating (perhaps) in respect of others (see further discussion in Chapter 10).

Higher Work Levels with Non-Managerial Responsibilities

A final point. We have stressed the necessary close relationship between work levels and levels of management. But is must also be stressed that none of the definitions of the various work levels offered above are couched in terms of managerial activity. Each is described in more general terms. This is important. It allows recognition of the fact that all front-line jobs, jobs shown at the bottom of organisation charts, are not necessarily pitched at level 1. Some may be at level 2; some even higher. Most factory workers may operate at level 1, but many salesmen may operate at level 2 (see further discussion in Chapter 8). Hospital porters may operate at level 1, but more senior doctors – still in direct contact with patients – may operate at level 3 (see further discussion in Chapter 9).

There are also many higher-level administrative or executive jobs, certainly up to the top of level 3 and sometimes even at level 4, where the management element, in terms of controlling numbers of direct subordinates, is minimal or wholly absent – like the assistant production director's job in the factory example just considered, or the deputy director's job in the public or voluntary agency example.

The work-level approach kills once and for all the simplistic idea that responsibility is purely a function of the number of other people managed. It provides a positive way of saying just what level of expectation and responsibility does exist in various jobs, whether managerial or not.

Conclusion

Adding ideas of work levels to the various models of authority relationships discussed in the previous chapter strengthens considerably the power of the design approach. It throws new light on optimum numbers of levels in any management chain. And it opens up the possibility of spelling out for either an individual post or some complete organisational unit, not only the general *kind* of output looked for (manufacturing, social work, insurance, personnel work, and so on), but the exact *level* of output in terms of the depth and comprehensiveness of impact on environment which is wanted.

Taking together these precise definitions of work levels and authority relationships, it becomes possible to specify *organisational requirements* in as much detail as is necessary to satisfy most practical needs, or overcome most potential uncertainties or confusions. But where do actual *people* come into all this with their different interests and motivations, aptitudes and abilities? How well do they fit with given organisational requirements, and vice versa? Whose task is it, not only to decide the organisational framework, but to align it to actual individuals and actual individuals to it? It is to this further and crucial aspect of any comprehensive approach to organisational design that we must next turn.

Notes

1. All these criticisms may be levelled at Urwick's early attempts to distinguish six

level of supervision (from lowest to highest) – 'oversight', 'executive supervision', 'general supervision', 'executive superintendence', 'administrative superintendence' and 'general superintendence'; also at Paterson's six-fold schema of decision bands (from lowest to highest) – 'defined', 'automatic', 'routine', 'interpretative', 'programming' and 'policy-making'. Beer's 'neurocybernetic model', which talks of the various control systems each of increasing complexity – systems 1 to 5 – necessary in any viable enterprise, is obviously broader in scope, but very abstract, and again, fails to provide any absolute scale. (See L. Urwick, *The Elements of Administration*, London, Pitman, 1943; T. T. Paterson, *Job Evaluation*, London, Business Books, 1972; S. Beers, *The Heart of Enterprise*, New York, Wiley, 1979.)

2. Jacques' ideas in this area, based on many years of consultancy and research, stem from the discovery of a close linkage between the generally perceived level of responsibility in any job and its 'time span of discretion' – broadly, the longest time-horizon within which its occupant has to function. He identifies at least seven distinct strata in organised work, with time-span ranges as follows: 0–3 months, basic shop-floor and clerical jobs more or less 'skilled', including working supervisors; 3–12 months, first full-managerial jobs; 1–2 years, typical second-level, or middle, management jobs; 2–5 years, typical senior management jobs; 5–10 years, typical jobs of chief executives of major operating companies; 10–20 years chief executives of groups of operating companies; 20 years and over, chief executives of major corporations. His own suggested definitions of the different qualities of work at these different strata are not couched, as ours are, in terms of required outputs or end-products, but in terms the different 'levels of abstraction' called for: perceptual concrete, imaginal concrete, imaginal scanning, and so on. See E. Jaques, *A General Theory of Bureaucracy*, London, Heinemann 1976, for a full statement of these and related ideas.

3. The original published statement of the work-level theory was in R. Rowbottom and D. Billis, 'The Stratification of Work and Organisational Design', *Human Relations*, vol. 30, no. 1, 1977, pp. 53–76.

4. We refer here to Herbert Simon's well-known distinction of 'programmed' and 'unprogrammed' work (H.A. Simon, *The New Science of Management Decision*, New York, Harper & Row, 1960). In our schema, even level 1 work is seen as typically involving some exercise of judgement or discretion, and in this sense 'unprogrammed'. Conversely, all higher-level work is seen as 'programmed' to some degree, but with objectives and constraints of an increasingly broader kind, as level succeeds level. Nevertheless, the upper boundary of level 1 does represent the limit of work that might, in principle, be readily automated or computerised. At level 2 and upwards, it is not just a case of having to deal with probabilities rather than facts, with incomplete definition rather than certainty. At such levels, work always involves the making of judgements about values and needs. It is difficult to imagine a computer on its own ever taking over such activity.

5. In public services like health and social welfare, the move from level 5 (or 6) to level 7 may be conceived as a shift from negatives to positives. At level 5 it may be argued that the prime business is that of tackling actual lacks or breakdowns of a significant kind from which individuals suffer – diseases, trauma, homelessness, inability to care for oneself, (See D. Billis, *Welfare Bureaucracies*, London, Heinemann, 1984, Chapter 4) and so on. Thus the focus is not really on health but ill-health, not on welfare but on social breakdown. (In education it ought perhaps to be on lack of the basic skills and knowledge to act as an adequate citizen.) At level 7, the concern changes. Broader preventive and developmental objectives now become appropriate. A concern with continuing and unlimited improvement in the health, well-being, education, and so on, of all the citizenry now becomes justified; a concern to be pursued by whatever means seem possible or desirable from any given political position.

4 Matching People, Jobs and Rewards

During prolonged discussions of organisational structures, participants in our various workshops and seminars have sometimes been heard to say in exasperation 'surely it is *people* that matter really, not organisation'. The reaction may be understandable but the logic is not. Any choice between people and organisation is unreal. Obviously, it is flesh-and-blood people, not organisational specifications or blueprints, that actually produce, create, get things done. But organisation – if it is good – can facilitate this productivity. It can remove obstacles, encourage cooperation, allow proper space for spontaneity, even indicate positively where initiative is expected. Good organisation must be good for those who work within it. It must be 'user-friendly', as it were. It must be suited to real individuals. And it must allow for the rich variety that exists in individual interest and talent – not just assume some lifeless image of the 'average' man or woman.

In this chapter we shall turn for a while to consider the human resource on which all organisation is based. Our particular concern will be the variation in people's abilities to tackle work of different levels. We shall consider the implications for recruitment, assessment, career planning, and pay. We shall explore how the idea of people having a particular level of ability accords with the reality that many jobs apparently span work at a number of different levels. Finally, we shall see how all this leads to a deeper appreciation of the key role of the main line-manager in maintaining a dynamic balance between people, jobs and rewards.

Level of Ability
The weakness in the general vocabulary for describing differences in required level of work, as opposed to differences in kind, has already been noted. The same applies when it comes to personal abilities. It is obvious that doctors, for example, have to have different skills than engineers, or engineers than accountants. Doctors have to know about

anatomy and physiology, and be able to diagnose disease; engineers have to understand the principles of dynamics, and be able to calculate stresses and strains; accountants have to know about company and taxation law, and be able to keep books. Differences in kind or field of ability can be described readily and in detail. But when it comes to distinguishing different *levels* of ability in any given field, it is much more difficult. What distinguishes a 'top' doctor from the run-of-the-mill practitioner, the chief engineer from one of his assistants, the finance director from the newly-qualified audit officer? Words like 'capable', 'intelligent', 'astute' or even 'experienced' have to stand in for a quality which is none of these things exactly, but all to some extent.

The existence of the work level schema itself provides a useful way of labelling this particular quality and registering with some precision a whole range of differences. It becomes possible, for example, to describe and distinguish two people with the same basic qualifications operating in the same field, one an individual of 'level 2 ability' – able to cope with complex open-ended situations in the field in question one at a time, and one of 'level 3 ability' – able to construct a systematic response to whole sequences of such situations.

But how does this particular component of ability vary from person to person? Is it fixed from birth or does it change? If so, in what way? In pursuing these further questions we may usefully refer to important ideas developed by Elliot Jaques.[1] Building on studies of a large number of actual career histories of people employed in a wide range of fields he came to the conclusion that the individual's ability to tackle work of various levels tends to develop over time according to one of a set of typical curves of the general form shown in Figure 4.1. (His levels effectively equate with ours, as mentioned before, although they are defined in a different way.) Now whether or not the particular curves he puts forward are exactly the right shape, and whether (more fundamentally) people do tend to stick to particular development curves throughout the whole of their working lives regardless of opportunity, education, and other environmental factors, we may leave as open questions. The most important thing is (we would suggest) the basic idea that the individual's ability to tackle work at different levels is in course of continuous development throughout his or her whole working life, at a rate which itself may vary at different stages. This puts the whole business of assessing people's practical abilities in a radically new perspective, and one which would seem to accord more closely with the realities of work and careers than any approach which attempts to assign to people fixed 'intelligent quotients' or whatever, assumed to be applicable through the whole of adult life.

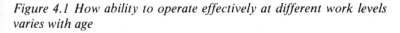

Figure 4.1 How ability to operate effectively at different work levels varies with age

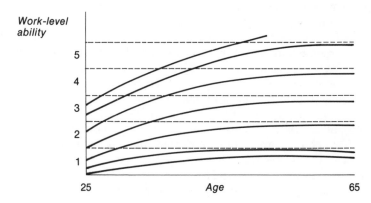

The other important idea which Jaques advances is that of the desirability of getting as close a match as possible between people's abilities and the levels of work in their actual jobs. This is something over and above the commonplace notion of people being employed in the right sort of work, a kind or field which best suits their own particular skills, interests and motivations – business, teaching, research, administration, or whatever it may be. His thesis is that, provided people are in the right basic field, they will be happiest and most productive when they are tackling work of a level which most closely matches their current capacities. With a level too far beyond them they will feel anxious, overstretched, unable to cope. With one too low they will feel bored, frustrated and underemployed. Over and above this, he suggests there is a third important factor: pay or reward. A pay rate for the individual which is significantly out of line either with expected work level or (if it is different) with current ability level, brings yet further tensions: resentment if the pay is too low, a measure of guilt (openly admitted or not) if it is too high.

Recruitment, Appraisal and Career Planning

Let us consider the practical implications of this extended range of ideas and in particular the notion of people's different and changing abilities to tackle work at different levels, for *recruitment, appraisal* and *career planning*.

As regards the first, the various work-level descriptions alone make it much easier, once it is clear what is actually required in any job at issue, to couch advertisements in terms likely to attract those of the right level of ability and deter those of too high, or low, ability. (They also make it easier to see where exactly any sexual or racial discrimination is arising in appointments.[2]) As regards actual selection, the descriptions provide specific and important criteria against which to judge individual applicants and around which to construct appropriate questions. (Applicants for level 3 jobs for example, may be posed questions designed to explore their ability to think in terms of general methods or procedures; applicants for level 4 jobs, questions to detect ability to think in terms of ranges of competing services and possible priorities amongst them.)

In both recruitment and selection it becomes easier to be specific, not just about what sort of *current* ability level is being demanded of applicants, but precisely what sort of *potential* is being looked for. There are always choices. In filling, say, a level 3 job, it may be hoped to get someone who, although their career may involve a modest growth in responsibility over time, will stay for many years in that level. Or it may be hoped to get someone who will rapidly push to level 4 or higher. The 'steady' sort of person right for the job, say, of office

Figure 4.2 Examples of possible match or mismatch between person and job

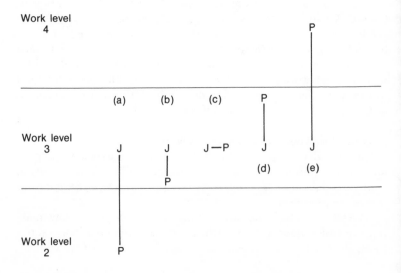

Figure 4.3 Different kinds of promotion

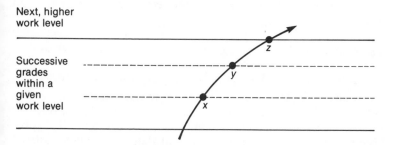

manager or head of maintenance will be very different from the 'high flier' desirable, say, for internal consultancy work, or for spearheading major developments.

As regards people in existing jobs, the idea of continuously developing abilities combined with the work-level descriptions allows a much more precise analysis of where people are up to at present, as well as where they are heading. It becomes possible to describe and distinguish a variety of 'overemployment' situations: a job at, say, mid-level 3 filled by a person of only level 2 ability (see Figure 4.2(a)) – a serious situation; or the same job filled by a person of bottom-level 3 ability (Figure 4.2(b)) – not so serious. It becomes possible to describe in precise terms a situation of balance: a mid-level 3 job filled by a person of mid-level 3 ability (Figure 4.2(c)). It becomes possible to describe and distinguish a number of 'underemployment' situations: a mid-level 3 job filled by a person of top-level 3 ability (Figure 4.2(d)) – not so serious; or filled by a person of level 4 ability – a much more serious misuse of talent (Figure 4.2(e)); and so on. Looking at potential as well as actual abilities it becomes possible to mark the difference, for instance, between, on the one hand, a person currently in level 2 but with judged potential to move to level 3 or even level 4 eventually, from on the other, his or her more competent and experienced colleague also in a level 2 job whose own potential, however, is a lesser one. And so on again.

As regards career planning, the approach emphasises the importance of distinguishing two different sorts of progression. Anytime in a person's career when he or she is changing from a job in one work level to another in the next – (z in Figure 4.3) – is likely to be particularly stressful. By definition, a qualitative jump is involved, and a completely different and more demanding set of expectations has to be coped with. By contrast, promotions from one grade of job to another within the same work level (*x* and *y* in Figure 4.3) are likely to be experienced as much easier. To give people promotions of the first kind when they are only ready for the second is obviously to court disaster.

The Possibility of a Person Operating at Several Work Levels at the Same Time

So far, it has been taken for granted that there is one unique work level in any given job. The point has now come to test that assumption. It is not the case that many jobs have in practice a number of different work levels implicit in them? Might this even be desirable? If so, what becomes of the notion of a close match of ability level and work level?

Several different situations must again be distinguished (see Figure 4.4). It is certainly the case that many higher-level jobs have elements of lower-level work attached to them; that they are downward-extending, as it were (Figure 4.4(a)). A common example is that of professional practitioners or first-line managers who (rightly or wrongly) have to carry out much of all of their own clerical work. But in such cases it is clear that the main focus is on the top-level work; the other might readily be delegated to assistants of some kind, were this to be judged expedient or economic.

Figure 4.4 Multi-level work

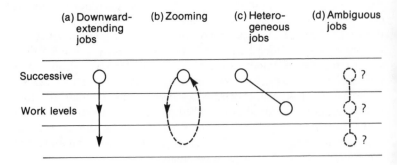

In the case of managerial jobs, and apparent mix of levels may mark something very different. There is an intrinsic mobility at work. Typical chief executives of large operating organisations, for example, will never spend all their time just considering the general field of activity, and creating policies and strategies for the shaping or reshaping of the general product range or service range – essential level 5 work. Inevitably, on occasion, they will be drawn into discussion of the details of particular services (level 4), particular systems or procedures (level 3), and particular problems with individual employees, customers, or clients (level 2).

It is a poor general who never visits the trenches. Wise managers make or take frequent opportunities to dip into work at lower levels in order to get a feel of the real issues and circumstances there. We call this *zooming* (Figure 4.4(b)). But if they fail to zoom back up having zoomed down, then something is wrong. One possibility is that the manager concerned is simply not up to his or her present job. In this case the zooming-down will represent a flight from what are felt as impossible demands. A person, for instance, of level 2 ability who is in level 3 job will be found to be continually involved in the intricate detail of particular cases and instances: it is what he can best do; the level of abstract through necessary to stand above the fray and see the whole process may be just beyond him. Another possibility is of course that some of the people at lower levels are themselves not up to their jobs. A third possibility is the one just considered: that the manager concerned is genuinely overloaded with work at lower levels. (In this case the answer may simply be the appointment of additional people to whom this lower work can be delegated: assistants, secretaries or whatever.)

Leaving all these last pathologies aside, zooming must be recognised as a normal, and indeed important, part of all managerial work. When properly occurring it involves not simply a zoom-down into a lower level of work but also a subsequent zoom-up, or return; the total sweep providing valuable concrete experience for the more abstract work to be carried out.

There are, then, downward-extending jobs with expectations of output at two or more levels. And there is zooming. In both, the main level of expected work is clear. In other cases, however, there may be less certainty about the matter. We have come across occasional examples of jobs which combine tasks in two quite distinct fields – acting as chief accountant and running a small transport section, for example – where the two parts appear to require work at quite distinct levels (Figure 4.4(c)). And we have frequently encountered jobs where the required work is not so much extended or heterogeneous in level as simply ambiguous or unclear (Figure 4.4(d)).

Whether or not situations of these last two types are tolerable in any given case, the basic point is this. Jobs may indeed, legitimately or otherwise, involve their occupants in exposure to, if not the actual execution of, elements at a variety of different work levels. But it is wrong to assume that in responding to these different levels the ability of the individual who is involved contracts or expands in some corresponding fashion – that one minute he or she is only capable of seeing aims and situations narrowly, the next far more broadly.

On the contrary, it is readily observable when people capable of operating at high levels get involved in work at a lower one, that they tackle it in a crucially different way, a way which constantly exhibits the characteristics of the higher-level approach. Where people with level 3 ability become involved in concrete situations needing their attention, these are rapidly seized on as illustrative instances of a general problem demanding a more systematic response. Where level 4 people become involved with particular ailing systems or procedures their interventions inevitably lead to considerations of how the benefits might be extended comprehensively throughout the organisation concerned.

What also follows it that it is not possible in the nature of things for people, even temporarily, to operate at a level of work above that of their currently developed ability. This is not to say that people at lower levels may not usefully be *involved* in work at higher levels, through membership, for example, of appropriate management teams, working parties or consultative committees (an issue to which we return in later chapters). Indeed there is a particularly strong case for such involvement where subordinates are judged to be well on the way to developing the ability to operate at the higher levels concerned. But such involvement is essentially in the nature of offering either specific contributions or criticisms, or more general approval or disapproval. Fully manifested ability at any level is the ability to take the overall view, assess all the factors, and come down to firm judgements or decisions with confidence and reliability. If any individual has not at any stage of his career attained or grown into such a capability in relation to any given (higher) level of work, then it cannot simply be willed into being to meet some particular occasion.

In summary, then, although some jobs may combine actual executive elements at more than one work level, and many may involve discussions at more than one work level, there will always be one highest level (if the situation is at all clear) for which responsibility for final output or outcome is assigned. It is this that determines the calibre of person required. It is here that the matching of level of work to level of ability becomes crucial.

Reward Systems
Having explored the idea of multi-level work we may return to the main theme: the matching of work levels, ability and rewards. We have

considered the relationship of the first two. Where does the third element, pay or reward, come into the picture? Should work level (as Elliot Jaques has argued) itself be the major determinant of pay? Or, are there other and equally important considerations?

We ourselves adopt a cautious approach to this topic. We are very conscious of the diverse and conflicting views which exist on the subject. There is indeed what might be called the 'job-evaluation approach', the idea that pay ought to be determined wholly by the intrinsic qualities of any work in question, including its level of responsibility. But there is also the idea that pay ought to be completely settled by 'going rates' – the market approach. There is the idea that pay ought to respond to individual or family needs and the varying cost of living – the welfare approach. There is the idea that pay ought to reflect actual achieved output or productivity – the incentive view.

To some extent it is possible to combine these approaches. Where large organisations wish to develop wide-ranging payment systems, they may start with a framework based on job evaluation and then modify it at various points by making adjustments for market pressures, welfare needs or incentive schemes. However, if the adjustments are too many or too great, the whole approach loses coherence.

In setting up any comprehensive payment systems for a whole range of different jobs, managerial and professional as well as manual and clerical, the basic approach is almost bound to be through some kind or other of job evaluation. And in any job-evaluation scheme itself, higher responsibility or higher work level (essentially the same thing) is bound to be given considerable weight, whatever allowance is made for things like bad working conditions or unsocial hours.[3]

This is not to deny the importance of work at low levels. Without the contributions of the millions of labourers, drivers, assemblers, clerks, storemen, cleaners, and so on, who operate at level 1, society would rapidly disintegrate. Nevertheless, with work only at this level, there could be no significant innovation or progress; no adaptation to new circumstances, or effective response to calamities. From this second viewpoint, work undoubtedly becomes of greater value to society level-by-level as broader vistas are taken into account and more-fundamental needs embraced. It seems self-evident that not everybody can work at higher levels. And given a comparative scarcity of ability to tackle high-level work, it seems probable that those gifted individuals who have such ability, all other things being acceptable, will always be accorded some special status or respect by their fellows.

However, the crucial issue is not status or prestige, but the allocation of material rewards. We note that higher-level jobs do tend to command more income in most modern societies. But as to what should be the proper range of differentials for this particular factor (let alone what should be the proper weight to give to the various other things mentioned above) we have ourselves no strong arguments to advance.

Where we would offer positive statements would be in two regards. The first is this. Large organisations often do find it convenient to relate particular jobs or positions to some overall structure of *grades*. Among other things, this allows the easier separation of across-the-board pay increases from pay increases for particular jobs, or pay increases for particular individuals; and it allows a more rational system for assigning perquisites. Where grading systems do exist, it is essential, as has been argued, to distinguish them from management structures. But there are a variety of reasons for relating them explicitly to work levels (as here defined).

Following this course, it will sometimes be possible to assign one grade to one whole work level. Often, however, it will be necessary to assign several grades to each work level in order to mark fine but significant differences in responsibility among different jobs at that level (see Figure 4.5). But either way, *so long as no grade crosses two work levels*, the possibility is avoided of any uncertainty – fatal, as just pointed out, to effective recruitment and selection – about what work level is actually required in any given job. Moreover, the possibility is reduced if not completely avoided of somebody's work becoming shifted from one work level to the next higher by accident or chance – a major transition for any person to cope with, as suggested above, even if and when they are ready for it. And the likelihood is reduced of managers finding at some point that they are, because of overlapping pay scales, paid less than some of their own subordinates – a situation which invariably, in our experience, generates grievance.

The explicit linking of grades to work levels has other potential benefits. It helps keep free of the pernicious tendency, particularly evident in the public sector, to grade jobs purely in terms of obvious numerical indices like numbers of staff to be managed, places or beds controlled, population to be served, or revenue to be handled, when what is really wanted is a salary to attract the sort of person likely to be able to make some required level of impact on the environment, regardless of other circumstances. It avoids the supposition, again only too frequent, that no 'front-line' job can be worth as much as any with a supervisory or managerial content. And it provides a common language for comparing differentials across different organisations in the same or different fields of work.[4]

The second and more fundamental point that we would wish to

Figure 4.5 Relating grades to work levels

```
Work
level              grade

                    etc
                 ----------
  3                 3B
                 ----------
                    3A
_____
                    etc
                 ----------
  2                 2B
                 ----------
                    2A
_____
                    etc
                 ----------
  1                 1B
                 ----------
                    1A
_____
```

make about pay, arises whether or not there is a grading system or indeed a systematic approach of any kind. It springs from the question of who, for any given individual in any given organisation, should be the key person in the allocation of any material rewards. As regards all those involved in straightforward employment work (leaving aside governors, directors, and the chief executives themselves) the proposition is that such ought to be the person who carries a main line-managerial relationship to the individual employee concerned. It will not necessarily be this person who determines the overall pay framework or policy (if any). But if there is any discretion in the system at all as to how pay is matched to individual performance, then it ought to be the main line-manager who makes the prime judgements on appropriate increments or decreases, rewards or penalties.

The Key Role of the Main Line-Manager in Matching Person, Job and Rewards

This brings us to a substantial conclusion. Throughout the chapter we have emphasised the need to get as good a match as possible between the work levels allocated to people and those of which they are capable

– their actual ability levels. Moreover, in paid jobs, some sort of positive relationship between expected work level (however modified by other factors) and reward level also seems desirable, as just discussed.

However, getting and keeping a balance between these three elements – work level, ability level, and reward level – is by no means simple. Material rewards can usually be quantified, but it is not so easy to measure exact work levels (varying as they do, not only across the main qualitative strata, but in significant degree within each). Nor is it easy to get any precise or reliable measure of individual ability levels. No element, moreover, is likely to stay fixed over any substantial period of time. The ability of the individual is likely, as suggested, to be constantly changing or developing at some greater or lesser rate as life experience generally accrues. The work level, even in a supposedly unchanged job, will often be varying independently, as new technologies are brought in, as pattern of demand changes, and as social and physical environments alter. Even pay levels, apparently fixed, will be constantly changing relative to others obtainable for the same work elsewhere, as well in terms of their buying power where inflation is in evidence.

In no way could the balancing of these elements be mechanically or automatically contrived. What is needed in respect of each individual employee is one person who can be making a continual appraisal of performance, ability and potential (zooming down as necessary in order to do so); making in consequence any appropriate change in exact level of responsibility allocated to each (within the general qualitative work level of the job concerned); and making or influencing accordingly any appropriate change in material rewards.

This, of course, merely restates the essential role of the main line-manager as specified in detail in Chapter 2. *It provides a broader conception of the essential task of the main line-manager in relation to his or her subordinates, as being responsible for contriving to keep at all times as close a match as circumstances allow between their abilities, the actual work allocated to them, and their rewards.* It is this function above all others that distinguishes the main line-managerial role from all other types discussed earlier – supervisory, coordinating, monitoring or whatever.

Of course, emphasising the role of main line-managers does not detract from the need for specialist personnel work. Good personnel managers, acting in support of main line-managers, can make their own important contribution to this central task of matching people, jobs and rewards. They can do much to improve methods of recruitment and selection. They can introduce better payment and appraisal systems. They can spearhead the development of more sophisticated approaches to job-structuring and organisational design. Above all, they can establish a climate in which awareness of all these matters becomes much sharper throughout the whole of their particular organisations.

Nor need it be assumed that main line-managers will all perform equally well in their particular and crucial part in the task concerned. Sometimes their decisions or recommendations on sensitive things like pay increases, regradings or dismissals will reveal obvious personal biases. Sometimes they will manifest plain and simple incompetence in handling work in this area. A necessary counterpart (we believe) to a managerial structure of the kind described here is a strongly developed *appeals or grievance procedure* of some kind. Effective executive organisation can never be run as a simple democracy; leading figures of real power and authority have to be identified. Nevertheless, from another point of view, all who are permanently employed in a given organisation become, in a sense, its 'citizens'. And, as in the civic state, they should have recourse to some separate system of justice when they feel badly done by, or ill-used.

Noting these last provisos, we return, however, to the main point. Organisations are groups of people. People, not money or material goods, constitute the basic resource. To exploit this resource to the full, to make full use (but not overuse) of its energy and creativity under constantly changing conditions, is the first task in any executive organisation. And in this task, the main line-manager should play the key part (which again shows why it is so important to get an effective structure of main managerial roles with neither too many levels nor too few).

Notes

1. See again E. Jaques, *A General Theory of Bureaucracy*, London, Heinemann, 1976.
2. Reference is frequently made to the barriers which prevent women or members of disfavoured ethnic groups from getting managerial or executive jobs. But such jobs can be pitched anywhere from level 2 to level 5 – or higher. Much more precision is needed if the issues are to be properly confronted. Our own impression is that women can readily achieve promotion to level 2 or level 3 jobs, particularly in fields like teaching, nursing, journalism or retailing, but experience major obstacles in getting jobs at level 4 or higher. On the other hand, the bar for coloured or black people may be lower. What proportion of the latter achieve jobs even in levels 2 or 3, in contrast to supervisory jobs at the top of level 1?
3. Job-evaluation schemes often pose other factors beyond the three mentioned (level of responsibility, bad working conditions and unsocial hours): things like complexity of decision-making; mental effort; required skill; required experience; and length of training necessary. But many or all of these must be questioned as independent factors. Is complexity of decision-making, or even mental effort, any different from work level? Are not required skills, experience and training referring

to what is looked for in the individual rather than the job, and is not the inclusion of these thus really double counting?

4. Public information about earnings and differentials is frequently categorised according to occupation, but rarely if ever according to level. For jobs which can be confidently assumed to rest wholly within level 1 – those of cleaners, copy-typists, machine-hands, etc. – this may not matter too much. But the work levels approach exposed the fatuity of posing questions like how much doctors earn on the average, or works managers, or architects, or company directors. The President of the Royal College of Surgeons is likely to earn vastly more than the new surgical house officer, and the managing director of a multinational corporation vastly more than the managing director of a small local business. Meaningful figures for earnings of occupational groups like these simply have to take account of differences in responsibilities. The work-level schema offers a practical way of doing so.

5 The Prime Design Decisions

Three sets of basic ideas have now been described, all of which have developed in the effort to understand better and to help resolve actual problems of various kinds commonly found in large-scale organisations. The first set consists of a range of model *authority relationships* – main line-managerial, supervisory, coordinating, and so on – of a detailed and precise kind. The second consists of an equally precise means of describing and modelling the vertical component of organisation, in the form of a fivefold (or sevenfold) range of *work levels*. The third are ideas about corresponding *ability levels*, levels which vary from individual to individual and (most importantly) levels which are constantly changing at some greater or lesser rate for each person over the course of his or her working life.

Already, certain of the relationships between the three sets of ideas have been explored. The interconnection between main line-managerial posts and work levels has been examined (with a resulting proposition that the optimum is just one post of such a kind per work level, as defined). There has been discussion of the relation between work levels and ability levels, and of the key role of main line-managers in trying to maintain a constant balance of the two.

We are now in the position to study more systematically how these various ideas, singly or together, may be put to use in the process of organisational design as a whole. In this chapter we shall look at five prime steps in the design of any executive organisation, which fall into a logical sequence as follows:

(1) *Decide basic expected work-level* – the exact kind or level of direct response that those at the front line, the factory workers, salesmen, service deliverers, and so on, are expected to make to their particular environments.
(2) *Decide highest expected work level* – the kind or level of impact that the organisation as a whole is required to make.

(3) *Settle main-management levels* – the optimum number and disposition for the organisation concerned.

(4) *Decide divisions or groupings* –how activities are best grouped into separate divisions, departments, sections or whatever, at each main-management level.

(5) *Deal with any excessive spans of control* (by various expedients to be described).

(6) *Determine staff and support roles* – the number and variety to give necessary guidance and support to the main managerial and operational system.

In the next chapter, a number of secondary or further issues of organisational design will be discussed.

Deciding the Basic Expected Work Level

What is the organisation expected to be doing at its front line, at its output end? It will usually be clear what *sort* of work is called for – manufacturing, selling, service delivery, teaching, consultancy or whatever. But what may well remain unconsidered or only half considered is the *level* of work; that is, the level of immediate impact required on the environment; the level of immediate response required to the needs of particular customers, clients and so on. *For most organisations, there will be a choice of three possible, and qualitatively different, basic expected work levels*: levels 1, 2 or 3. Different answers will be called for in different cases. In production work, for example, the usual assumption would be that front-line workers are all expected to operate in a prescribed output (level 1) mode. However, there may be some more highly-skilled production work where a situational response (level 2) mode is really required. In other areas the choices may be far more open. For front-line members of sales organisations there may be many, particularly in retailing, who are only expected to make a level 1 response to the needs of customers. However, there may be many again, particular travelling representatives, who are expected to make a level 2 response. There may be some, like representatives of computer-systems firms, or sellers of complex insurance and financial packages, who are expected to work at level 3. In services like social work, policing, teaching or nursing there may be a case for a basic front-line response at level 2, but one strongly supported by a level 1 output provided by separate categories of staff. In activities like higher education, management consultancy, or industrial design, there may be a requirement for virtually all in the front line to be capable of making a level 3 response to the needs of their clientele.

Many of the examples just mentioned are considered in more detail in Part Two. In general, the choice of basic expected work level – and it is in the end a choice – is one of the most important decisions in any organisation.

Deciding the Highest Expected Work Level

Equally important, of course, is the question of what the organisation as a whole is supposed to be doing. Again, there will be a distinction between kind of work and level. Again, the first will usually, although not always, be tolerably clear: whether the organisation concerned is supposed, say, to be producing chemicals, or mounting an outer-space programme, or dealing with youth unemployment. But the spread and depth of impact that the enterprise as a whole is expected to make in the world may need to be spelt out more carefully.

Here again, work-level descriptions allow the choices to be presented in a clear-cut way. (The descriptions are, as pointed out before, in absolute, not relative, terms.) A new youth agency, for example, might be expected merely to provide a systematic flow of services of some given kind at some given location or office (level 3); or it might be expected to provide a comprehensive range of established services throughout the whole of some given district or region (level 4); or it might be expected to tackle the broad field of need in some given district or region in a radical way, developing quite new ranges of services if necessary (level 5). (Further examples of the choices in specific settings are considered in Part Two.)

In talking of highest expected work level it should be noted that what is being described is in fact the work level expected of the chief executive or executives. The ultimate authority in any organisation will usually reside in a governing body of some kind – the board of directors of a commercial company, the governing committee of a voluntary body, a statutory public authority, or whatever. But it is not such bodies that are charged with carrying out the highest levels of executive work. They undoubtedly do have to undertake smaller-scale executive acts of their own, such as appointing senior staff or ensuring that particular meetings and discussions are carried through effectively. But their essential function is that of setting or sanctioning policy for the rest of the organisation: the broad directions in which the main body of executive activities should proceed, and the major priorities and constraints which should be observed.[1] Put another way, if the expected work level of the chief executive is x, it is a fundamental error to assume that the work level of the governing body is $(x + 1)$.

Usually, for any free-standing operating organisation, the choice of highest expected work will be level 3, 4 or 5. Below level 3 an organisation as such can hardly be said to exist. Above level 5 what is in view is not one but a whole complex of operating organisations.

A level 3 operating organisation will, as already indicated, be rooted in one particular location. Products or services may be marginally improved or cheapened as time goes by, but nothing more dramatic can be expected. By contrast, a level 4 organisation will be attempting to respond to the needs of a whole territory or society, not just to what happens at a particular location. Various offices, workshops or other facilities will be being opened or closed from time to time in a purposeful way. There may still be no very radical innovation in products or services, but a comprehensive range of some kind is now expected to be on offer. A level 5 organisation will also be attempting to respond to the needs of some complete territory or society, but will now offer, within its particular field, the possibility of radical change or innovation in product or service. It will thus be tackling an operational brief of the highest or most general kind.

Settling the Number of Main Management-Levels

Given, in any organisation, a clear decision about both the basic, and the highest, expected work levels, the optimum number of main management levels follows readily. As discussed in Chapter 3, the guiding principle is *one main line-management post per work level (above the first)*. Thus, with basic work at level 1 and highest work at level 5, the optimum is four main management levels; with basic work at level 2 and highest work at level 4, the optimum is two main management levels, and so on. Having more management levels than the optimum brings (as earlier discussed) characteristic and deep-rooted problems. So in general, does having less than the optimum number (the particular case of 'personal assistants' – examined later in this chapter – apart).

A special issue may be noted in the management of certain kinds of professional staff who can legitimately claim particular areas of autonomy, either for each individual practitioner of appropriate status (as in the case of senior hospital doctors, or established university lecturers) or for the professional group in general (as currently in the case for publicly employed social workers and nurses). In such cases, the full range of authority in the main line-managerial role, as defined earlier, may simply not be available for use at all levels. It is not currently acceptable, for example, for medical consultants working in the British National Health Service to be given instructions on particular treatments to be administered to particular patients. But this does not mean that no management of their work of any kind is necessary. If the basic expected work in the individual consultant job is say level 3, there is a clear need for somebody to undertake the necessary level 4 work, albeit acting in certain regards with co-ordinating and monitoring authority rather than full main line-managerial authority. The person or body concerned might be drawn from the ranks of professional administrators or managers, or from amongst the consultants themselves. In any level 5 health-service operating unit there would also be a need to settle who was responsible for the necessary level 5 management work in respect of consultants.

In general, separate bodies, individual or collective, exercising extensive management functions, are needed at each higher level where professionals with a significant degree of autonomy are employed just as much as where they are not (for further discussion see Chapter 9 and 11).

Deciding Divisions or Groupings at Each Level

Once the basic and highest expected work levels and the optimum number of main management-levels have been settled, the next step is to decide the best divisions or groupings of activities at each. This is the right order to tackle things: there can be no question of getting a effective lateral structure if the backbone is wrong.

Possible *bases* for grouping or lateral division, at any level of organisation, have been well explored by various writers over the years, although no two offer exactly the same list. Major alternatives include division by *place*, by *time*, by *clientele*, by *function*, by *product or service*, and by *project* or *programme*. Various criteria for choice have been identified. Resultant groups or divisions should, for example, serve to protect or develop expertise as far as possible. They should be self-contained as far as possible. They should be of broadly commensurate size or importance. (Some of these criteria may of course conflict in practice.[2])

As regards choosing among the various bases listed above, no very reliable propositions seem yet to have been developed. All that can be said with confidence is that no one basis is best in all cases. It should be noted that there is no bar to using a mixture of bases at any given level. The organisation of a retailing business might well, for example, be split into four main parts: three large geographically separate department stores (organisation by place), and one central purchasing unit (organisation by function). A local health service might well be divided into four main units: two general hospitals (organisation by place), one unit for all services for the mentally ill (organisation by client grouping) and one unit of so-called community services (organisation by function).

Optimum grouping may then be mixed, and depends strongly on particular circumstances. Work level ideas do, however, throw further light on the subject. It would appear, for example, that organisation by *time* is a possibility only at relatively low levels. Typical shift work in factories or hospitals, for instance, seems to demand no higher than a level 2 approach. Organisation by *function* is always a strong option at work levels 1, 2 and 3 where the maintenance and development of particular professional or craft skills is often of paramount importance. But at higher levels the strong interdependency which usually accompanies functional splits is much less tolerable. It is for this reason that, in commerce and industry, the creation of *product-group* or *service* divisions becomes an increasingly attractive proposition at level 4 and above (see further discussion in Chapter 6). Organisation by *project* (or *programme*) appears to be an option most frequently suited to middle work levels, more specifically to levels 2, 3 or 4. However, such organisation, being intrinsically short-lived usually requires a backing of some more permanent kind (see the reference to 'matrix' organisation below). As regards the other two main bases, organisation by *place* or by *clientele*, both seem possible at all levels from level 1 upwards.

One other general point may be noted. Whatever the prime basis of division chosen at any level, the demands of other possible bases can never be completely ignored. If *place* is chosen as the prime basis of division, the special needs of different *client groups* cannot be gainsaid. If *product* is chosen, the demands for some coordination by *function* still hold force. And so on. *What frequently follows is a type of organisation now commonly known as 'matrix', in which separate organisational strands exist in two (or more) dimensions.* Some of the further design issues involved here will be explored in Chapter 6.

Dealing with Unwieldy Spans of Control

The number of main management levels having been settled, and the divisions or groupings of activities at each, it will now become evident just how many subordinates each main line-manager has to oversee, that is, just how large are the spans of control. Conventional approaches to the design of management systems often start in fact with consideration of this latter. They reverse the procedure just described, looking first at optimum spans and then proceeding to see the implications for the number of main management levels required, inserting extra levels to reduce over-large spans as necessary.

There are two major drawbacks to this way of doing things. The first is in knowing exactly what does constitute an optimum span – should it be three, seven, ten or how many? *Almost a century of discussion has failed to reveal any golden number for either the maximum or the optimum that any one person can supervise.* It all turns out to be heavily dependent on circumstances. Sometimes as many as forty turn out to be possible, at others as few as four.[3] A criterion that can vary so greatly is really no help at all. The second drawback is, of course, that inserting extra management levels in an arbitrary fashion is likely to do untold damage to the operation of the whole management system, in ways which have now been thoroughly exposed.

However, neither of these things means that spans of control themselves are of no significance. Starting (as we have done) with a prime concern for optimum numbers of levels, it is clearly possible to land up with unwieldy spans at certain points, particularly in more labour-intensive undertakings. 'Unwieldy' here would imply no special number, but merely a judgement that some particular main line-manager would simply have too many direct subordinates to look after, bearing in mind the particular degree of interaction between them, the particular kind and regularity of demands they themselves are likely to throw up, demands on the manager from other quarters, and so on.

Given an unwieldy span of control at any point there are in fact three other possible lines for improvement, short of inserting additional management levels (with all the attendant problems). In some cases it may be possible to combine subordinate posts, thus immediately reducing the numbers to be overseen (the danger of course is that this may simply overload the subordinate staff concerned either directly or, if they themselves are managers, by increasing their own spans of control to unacceptable figures.) In other cases it may be possible simply to split off some or all of the staff or staff sections to be managed or supervised (although this, too, may merely switch the span-of-control problem elsewhere).

The third and more generally applicable possibility for helping to deal with unwieldy spans of control is simply to provide appropriate support staff to the manager concerned: staff who can help by dealing authoritatively with many minor problems relating to subordinates' work which would otherwise demand his or her full attention. Where large numbers of factory, office or service staff at level 1 have to be managed, then posts of the kind described in Chapter 2 as 'supervisory' may be the answer (see Figure 5.1(a)). Here supervisors, each in charge of a particular group of staff, can screen the main line-manager from a host of routine matters to do with things like inducting newcomers, assigning specific tasks, dealing with small problems or breakdowns, checking on discipline, and so on. (Major issues such as judging the general capability of staff members, deciding what level of responsibilities to allocate to them, and influencing rewards must still, of course, rest with the main line-manager.)

At higher levels of work, the introduction of one or more posts of a 'staff-officer' type can often help a heavily burdened manager (see Figure 5.1(b)). Properly established staff-officers are not simply to be seen as advisers, but able to give clear instructions in their own right.[4] Within policies and directions set by the main line-manager, they will act with co-ordinating and monitoring authority, as earlier defined. If there is more than one staff officer, each will usually deal with a particular field of issues affecting all subordinate staff – in contrast to supervisors, who typically deal with all issues affecting one particular group of staff. Personnel work is one common field of staff work. Planning and scheduling work is another.

Figure 5.1 Ways of reducing the burden of extended spans of control on main line-managers through the creation of support posts

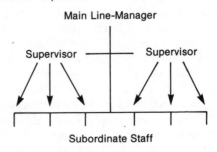

(a) By the creation of 'supervisors'

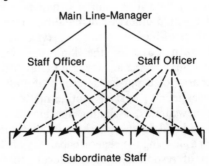

(b) By the creation of 'staff officers' in monitoring and co-ordinating roles

No modern army would dream of operating without a proper complement of staff officers. Industry, commerce, and the public services all seem (in our experience) curiously backward in adopting this useful organisational expedient. Often however, so-called 'assistants' or 'deputies' act close to such a role in practice.

The use of either supervisors or staff officers to help with over-large spans of control does bring another layer of authority into the organisation. But it does not create another layer of management, as we have been at pains to describe it, and does not, therefore, weaken a structure in which each main management-level commands its own distinct level of work.

Deciding Necessary Staff and Support Structures

We have already started upon the final step in the prime design process – deciding the necessary staff and support structure. Logically, this issue must come after the ones previously discussed. No amount of playing around with supporting structures can ameliorate either a management hierarchy or an activity grouping that is basically weak in some way. All it is likely to do is add to the general cost and confusion.

There may be a number of good reasons for adding staff and support posts, and a variety of different kinds of post are possible. As we have just seen, one of the prime reasons for introducing such posts is to help main line-managers deal with an otherwise excessive burden of oversight and control. The result can be either supervisory or staff-officer posts. Other support posts may often be created where, for reasons of expertise or economy, it is decided to bring together certain specialist facilities – to provide a centralised typing pool for example, or to provide a central computing, recruitment or maintenance facility. Here, the result will be one or a series of 'service' roles, as defined in Chapter 2. Sometimes service and staff-officer roles may be combined, as, for example, where personnel officers provide specific recruitment or training services as well as being involved in policy development and implementation.

Beyond this, there may be need to provide assistance of a more general kind at certain points, either to main line-managers or to certain categories of front-line staff. As regards the latter, we have already seen that the basic expected work of the front-line staff is not always level 1. Often it will be level 2, occasionally even level 3. However, the fact that the occupant of a front-line post (a particular salesman perhaps, or research officer, or professional nurse or social worker) is expected to operate at level 2 does not mean that there will be no level 1 work to be done. Higher levels of work always breed lower levels, so to speak – there are never any that can be missed out.

The question is whether, in any given case, it is sensible to leave the role as a downwards-extending one (of the kind described in Chapter 4), or whether to hive off some of the level 1 parts into an additional post, to be filled by an aide or assistant of some sort (as shown in Figure 5.2(a)). There is no general answer. Each case has to be judged according to its own merits.

Figure 5.2 Possible patterns of assistant posts to high-level 'front-line' workers

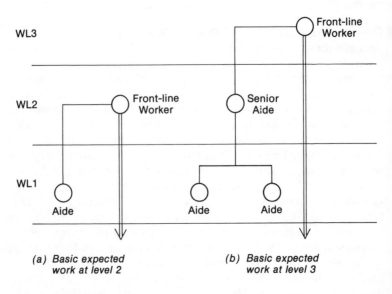

(a) *Basic expected work at level 2*

(b) *Basic expected work at level 3*

Where front-line posts are at level 3 (specialist consultants or designers, for example) there is a question not only of hiving off level 1 components but also level 2. In this case a small hierarchy of assistants might result, a senior aide at level 2 managing one or more junior aides at level 1 (Figure 5.2(b)). The important thing to emphasise here, however, is that any aides at level 1 and 2 are in this case to assist in the production of output at level 3. (This is very different from a typical factory system, for example, where staff at level 2 and 3 are typically there to manage a flow of output at level 1.)

As regards assistance to main line-managers, this may be required for a variety of reasons apart from that already considered (namely to provide help in supervising, monitoring or coordinating the work of numerous subordinates). The managers concerned may simply need secretarial support, or somebody to carry out *ad hoc* investigations or collect information. They may need help in producing detailed plans. They may need somebody to deputise for them. And so on.

Many of these functions may be combined, but a major distinction must be observed between assistants who operate in the immediate work level down from the manager and those who operate at lower work levels still. The latter will often be called 'secretaries' or 'personal assistants' or 'assistants to'. The former will carry quite a different status. Assuming that they are not themselves main line-managers in charge of major operational or service functions they will usually (in our experience) tend to carry significant co-ordinating or monitoring responsibilities and authority. Deputies are in a special position, and demand a separate word.

Deputies
There appears a strong tendency when people are actually trying to show operative work levels in organisation charts, for them to plot deputies (or even senior assistants) in the same band or level as their bosses. No doubt this says something about the accustomed status of centrally-based staff and the magic that often accrues from simply being in close social and spatial contact with the ultimate source of authority. Nevertheless, it is illogical. The grade of the deputy post may be very close to that of the boss. But for optimum conditions the deputy, like all others who work for a particular boss, should be operating at a lower work level.

It could well be, in a particular case, that the deputy happens to be capable of doing his or her boss's job. It may often be the case that the deputy, though not yet quite at that point, is well on the way to it. But personal ability and expected work level are different things. Of course, deputies will tend to get involved in some degree in all the issues which concern their bosses. They may aid them, advise them, on occasion speak for them, on almost any matter. But responsibility for the final judgements and the final decisions on all top-level matters must rest solely with the bosses.

What, then, of the common supposition that deputies are expected to take over fully the jobs of their bosses when the latter are for some reason absent? This, we suggest, is a highly simplistic picture. Usually, in the absence of the boss, the task of the deputy will be to deal only with urgent operational matters. It will be precisely the longer-term, more strategic, issues – that is, the essence of the higher-level work – that he or she will not be expected to take significant action upon. Necessary fire-fighting will have to be done. But no boss will expect to come back after a short absence to find that the person deputising has fundamentally reorganised things, switched staff around or set a new policy framework. The length of time that the boss is expected to be away is, however, crucial. In the case of prolonged absence, deputising as just described, moves gradually into a full-scale 'acting' role, with more and more elements of the higher-level work necessarily being taken up. But this is a different matter.

Conclusion

A general sequence of steps for dealing with the prime design issues in executive organisation has now been traced out. Most fundamental are the choices about the kinds or qualities of impact which any given organisation is required to make on its environment, overall and in its direct front-line operation. The work-level descriptions allow decisions on these issues to be stated in explicit terms of the highest expected work level and the basic expected work level, respectively. On the principle of one main management level per work level, the vertical dimension of the management structure then readily follows.

Important decisions must next be made about the best grouping of functions or activities at each level. There is in general no one best way, but at least some of the choices and criteria can be spelt out. Finally, there is necessary staff and support structure to be added, one of whose purposes is to help deal with excessive spans of control.

With these steps taken, the broad shape of the executive structure becomes clear. Moveover, before these matters are dealt with, no others can be satisfactorily considered. But other aspects of organisational design, and important ones, there certainly are. These may be a need for management teams and coordinating committees of various kinds. There is the possible use of project groups and matrix organisation. There are things like joint consultative councils and worker-directors to be considered; also (at the other end of the organisation) job enrichment and various schemes for involving shop-floor workers more directly in management. There is the whole question of decentralisation to be considered. To these broader issues of teamwork, decentralisation, and participation we next turn.

Notes

1. In many commercial organisations the division between governing and executive functions is complicated by the fact that top executives – presidents, vice-presidents, managing directors, sales directors, and so on – are often themselves members of the governing body. But in such circumstances, each person concerned really has to be seen as carrying out two distinct roles, an executive one and a governing one, each with its own distinct responsibilities, authority, and expectations of behaviour. In the sphere of public agencies the division is usually more evident with different

sets of people doing the two jobs. It then becomes obvious that not every member of, for example, the elected council of a local authority, needs to be of very high work-level capability. It is possible in such fields for people of the right general outlook and experience to act quite adequately as setters or sanctioners of broad social policies, even though their own executive abilities may be no higher than level 2 or level 3, and even though many of the officers whose work is to be overseen may be in jobs with level 4 or 5 expectations.

2. For discussions of lateral divison, see for example, R. Stewart, *The Reality of Organisations*, London, Macmillan, 1970; H. Mintzberg, *The Structuring of Organisation*, Englewood Cliffs, NJ, Prentice Hall, 1979; H.D. Koontz, C. J. O'Donnell and H. Weihrich, *Management*, New York, McGraw Hill, 1980; and J. Child, *Organisation*, New York, Harper & Row, 1984.

3. The famous case is that of the Sears Roebuck Company in the United States, which reported in the 1950s that its mail-order organisation worked quite happily with spans of control at some levels of up to forty people (J. C. Worthy, *Big Business and Free Men*, New York, Harper Bros, 1959). For a general discussion of spans of control, see Child, *Organisation*.

4. The idea that all staff posts are essentially advisory still lingers in many influential texts – see, for example, Koontz, O'Donnell and Weihrich, *Management*. Others take a more realistic view. Even so, it is common for writers on the subject to hedge bets a little by talking about those in staff posts 'issuing instructions in the chief's name' or 'relying on the authority of expertise'. The root of the difficulty is the failure to get away from the idea, whose falsity was exposed in Chapter 2, that organisational authority is only of one kind, the authority to 'instruct'.

6 Teamwork, Decentralisation and Participation

According to much of the existing literature on organisation it would appear necessary at some point to make a major choice between two fundamentally different approaches, or at least between two different organisational types. The first is one often described as bureaucratic, hierarchic, or mechanistic; a type associated with Max Weber, Frederick Winslow Taylor, Henri Fayol and other turn-of-the-century theorists and practitioners. The second is given different names by different people, although the detailed descriptions have much in common. Douglas McGregor's term is 'Theory Y'; Burns and Stalker talk of 'organic' organisation; Mintzberg describes what he calls 'adhocracies'. Others again speak of open-system organisation, polyarchy, self-adaptive organisation, clover-leaf organisation, and so on.[1]

Although some writers have described types beyond two, and many have been at pains to stress that there are no absolutely right forms, only best ones for particular circumstances, the general impression is none the less of a simple duality of new and old, better and worse. The characteristics most usually associated with the two broad types, 'bureaucratic' and 'non-bureaucratic' as they might be called, may be summarised, and contrasted, as shown in Table 6.1. Now, adopting this view of things, it might seem that the design approach which has been being developed so far, with its frequent reference to hierarchies of work levels and different kinds of authority relations pertained only to bureaucratic organisation, and therefore to only one (and not particularly attractive) type. But such a conclusion would be false.

The approach described has in fact developed from work in organisations of the widest variety of kinds: service and manufacturing, commercial and industrial, public and private, large and small. Some of these organisations were undoubtedly innovative, open and forward-looking; others rather the reverse. Were any division of 'bureaucratic' and 'non-bureaucratic' to have been applied, some

Table 6.1 Broad images of 'bureaucratic' and 'non-bureaucratic' organisations current in the management literature

Bureaucratic organisations are	Non-bureaucratic organisations are
hierarchic	non-hierarchic or matrix-structured
authoritarian	participative or democratic
passive	innovative
individualistic	team-orientated
centralised	decentralised

would have fallen in the first category and others in the second. But our design approach has had direct relevance to all.

Does indeed the simple distinction between 'bureaucratic' and 'non-bureaucratic' organisation (or similar) have any real practical utility? We strongly doubt it (the issue is returned to at the end of this chapter). However, what cannot be in any doubt is the significance of the specific topics raised in the course of defining the two types: *hierarchy* and its possible modification or reduction; the issue of management *style*, authoritarian or other; *innovation and response to environment*; the development of effective *teamwork*; the use of *matrix organisation*, appropriate degree of *decentralisation*; the whole question of *employee participation*. On the contrary, all these things are of great interest in both organisational design and operation.

In this chapter we shall be looking at just these subjects. Our aim will not be to discuss them exhaustively but (in keeping with the central theme of the book) to expose the *structural options* behind each. We shall emphasise, whatever else may be done to reduce hierarchy in a general sense, how issues of different expected work levels inevitably remain, demanding some proper organisational response. We shall note how structural issues of authority relationships emerge in organisations both 'authoritarian' and 'participative' in general style or culture (and some of the ways, moreover, in which well-designed structures can actually promote better, more-relaxed styles). We shall mark the real range of choices behind the apparent simplicities of 'innovative' or 'non-innovative' organisations. We shall show some of the options behind supposedly straightforward ideas of teamwork, matrix organisation and decentralisation (or divisionalisation). We shall reveal various of the structural issues inherent in any philosophy of greater employee participation.

How Far Hierarchy May Be Dispensed With

Let us start with the question of hierarchy and how far it may be dispensed with. Many new approaches to organisation maintain that the whole notion of hierarchy is now outmoded. If 'hierarchic' is taken as a shorthand for all that is authoritarian, rigid, unchanging, petty-bureaucratic and status-obsessed, then the sentiment is one with which we are in full agreement. But if the proposition is that there can be new forms for organised human activity on any substantial scale in which all differences in levels of allocated work are systematically abolished, or for that matter, all differences in authority, then we would beg to differ.

Our contention throughout has been that, within organised executive action of significant scale, not only are there inevitable differences in the *kinds* of work to be undertaken by various participants but necessary differences in the *levels*. Indeed, we would claim that, until some reasonable understanding is reached about the latter just as much as about the former, it is doubtful how far effective organisation can be said to exist at all. If, for example, the occupant of a post of so-called engineer has literally no idea whether he is simply expected to continue manufacturing products of established kinds by established methods, or to be developing over time quite new products and methods, or to be creating gradually a whole new design capacity or productive facility to meet the demands of the future, then he is in no position to act in any concert at all with his fellows, however broadly or flexibly.

We have also stressed that differences in pay and status are one thing, whilst different levels of work are another thing again (although it is our hypothesis that differences in authority, however circumscribed, must inevitably accompany the latter). Even in the most open and egalitarian organisation where all dress the same, share the same conditions, receive the same rewards and regard each other as true brothers and sisters, the ultimate issue remains of who is to tackle work of any given complexity and their capability for doing so. It never goes away in organised executive action. Radical approaches to organisation and management may imply all manner of important differences in practice or outlook from so-called 'hierarchic' structures. But they do not do away with the need to respond to distinctions in the various required work levels. And in this sense, at least, regardless of what else may be changed, they leave hierarchy intact.

Having said this, two important points should be noted. The first is that executive activity is not everything. On the contrary, there is an evident need in all enterprises for separate institutions of some kind to settle the overall framework of policies, constraints and agreements within which executive action is to take place. We have at an earlier point touched upon governing bodies and their policy-making role. But the works councils and other consultative or negotiating bodies often found in large organisations at least, come in the same category. Some such machinery is clearly necessary and does indeed stand apart from the mainstream of executive activity and its associated hierarchy of work. (We return to this matter later in this chapter.)

The second point is that, in emphasising the inevitability of some broadly hierarchic system for executive work on any significant scale, we nevertheless do not suggest that there is, in Frederick Winslow Taylor's famous phrase, 'one best way' to organise. On the contrary, we ourselves are firm believers in a 'contingency' approach[2] – always provided that practical choices are properly developed. A variety of forms can be appropriate according to circumstances: sometimes organisation by product, sometimes by function, place, clientele, or time; sometimes the employment of straightforward managers, sometimes the use (as well as or instead of these) of staff officers, supervisors, or others in coordinating or monitoring roles of some kind; sometimes the development of close-knit teamwork, sometimes reliance on looser networks; sometimes the granting of advanced degrees of professional autonomy, sometimes not; sometimes the promotion of collective discussions through meetings and committees, sometimes emphasis on individual initiative; and so on. There is also a further diversity which arises from possible variations in management *style* within any given structure, an issue to which we now turn.

Management Style

Much of the talk about new approaches to management is not primarily about organisation structures in the sense of levels, roles and relationships. It is about styles, values, or cultures. When Douglas McGregor years ago introduced his famous Theory X and Y,[3] he was really contrasting two styles of management: the first based on the assumption that people are naturally lazy and can only be brought to work by the use of frequent sticks and carrots; the second based on the assumption that they are naturally active and creative, if only they can be encouraged to develop this. He never suggested that people called managers were unnecessary. He was not attacking *authority* as such, but *authoritarianism*. And when, twenty years later, Peters and Waterman talked about the characteristics of excellent firms, they concentrated heavily again upon basic attitudes and values: a willingness to risk and experiment; a real concern for employees as people; a genuine desire to serve the customer, and so on.[4]

Appropriate attitudes and values are an important feature of good management, perhaps the most important. But in themselves they do not say anything about accompanying structures. Systems which at certain points employ strong and well-defined relationships of manager and subordinate are not necessarily characterised by authoritarianism, rigidity, mistrust and fear. And systems which go out of their way to deny that managers have any special responsibility or authority are not necessarily (as all students of radical experiments well know) marked by genuine democracy, participation and openness.

Indeed, one can go further. It may well be that it is just those managers whose roles are adequately defined, and suitably separated in terms of work level from those of their subordinates (neither too near nor too far) who are in the best position to adopt a relaxed style of interaction. By contrast, it may often be those managers in ill-defined roles, perhaps scarcely differentiated in ability and real power from many of their so-called subordinates, who will be most tempted to retreat into browbeating, secrecy, and manipulative tactics in order to protect their status. Where hierarchic management structures are necessary, proper attention to work levels can actually improve the likelihood of developing a good culture or climate.

Innovation and Response to Environment
In terms of the two types described earlier, non-bureaucratic organisations are portrayed as innovative and able to respond to turbulence and change. By contrast, bureaucratic organisations are viewed as relatively static in outlook and poor at dealing with complex or demanding environments.[5] Since bureaucratic organisations are also characterised as hierarchic the implication is clear: anything that is hierarchic is also likely to be non-innovative and non-responsive!

Again, if 'hierarchy' is taken as an umbrella term for all that is passive, rigid, or authoritarian, then there is little more to be said. But if the view is taken – as here – that management hierarchies are basically about differences in levels of work, then the whole perspective changes completely.

As has been stressed at many points, the work levels schema is a way of categorising work precisely in terms of the differing extent of innovation expected, and response to environment required. The basic suggestion is that all human works calls in some degree for the use of judgement and initiative and not just slavish reaction. Moreover, no environment can be simply and finally categorised as turbulent or placid; so much depends on how it is viewed. High-level jobs are precisely those in which more fundamental innovation is demanded, a deeper slice of surrounding society and space is to be taken into account, a longer time perspective assumed. The shop-floor inspector who judges that some slightly defective batch of materials will nevertheless just pass muster for the particular job in hand; the buyer whose sixth sense now tells him to try to procure the materials in question from some new source; the director who decides that the time is coming for the firm to think of manufacturing these particular materials for themselves; all these people are making some positive response to signals of environmental disturbance, but it is a very different kind of response at the different levels.

We have also stressed before that the way in which any hierarchic system as a whole behaves depends markedly upon the expectations in the topmost posts – assuming of course that they are filled with people of commensurate ability. An organisation in which the top post is level 3 cannot be expected to respond to the world in a level 4 way. An organisation with top post or posts at level 5 may well appear more 'organic', that is, able to respond in a more creative and flexible way to its environment, than one which has no posts (or people) beyond level 4.

Teamwork

There can be little question of the importance in reality of teamwork in all organisations, so-called bureaucratic or otherwise. Commonly, however, there is quite insufficient attention devoted to the internal structures of teams. The general impression is often left, if not explicitly stated, that teamwork by its nature always demands inter-action between equals without any exercise whatever of authority. But this is simply not true. And the failure to observe possible differences in internal structure is often (in our experience) a potent source of conflict and confusion.

In teams, for example, where a main line-manager A who is expected to operate at one work level, meets regularly with his or her subordinates B1, B2, etc., who are expected to operate at the next lower work level (see Figure 6.1), final authority will logically remain with the former. The purpose of such meetings will presumably be to enter freely into collective discussion of current issues, prospects and policies. If a real team-like atmosphere is to be generated, A will have for much of the time to relinquish his predominant role: stand back a little, as it were; encourage B1, B2, etc., to join in freely and sponta-neously; refrain from excessive control. But given that A is expected to take a broader and deeper view than the others (and always assuming that he has an enhanced capability to match), then a time must come when he must reassert his authority by saying, 'let us settle for this or that' or 'let us pursue this more deeply' or (simply) 'let us move on'. If necessary, he may have on occasion to ignore some consensus which is emerging quite strongly amongst the rest. Certainly if A is an accountable manager it will be confusing to allow any idea that his views might be vetoed or outvoted by his subordinates.

Figure 6.1

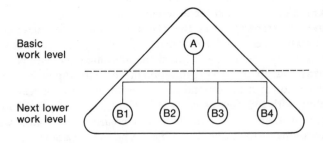

An extended and interlocking chain of such management teams, as shown in Figure 6.2, can in fact provide an extremely powerful and effective piece of organisation: one which combines focused accountability and leadership with a high degree of teamwork and communication, and one which provides a useful chain of settings in which to develop successive levels of policy.[6] However, it can be seen that such management teams must themselves be positioned exactly one work level apart. Should additional teams be created based on superfluous levels in the management structure, then they will at best merely echo the debate in teams led by those in strong management posts and, at worst, create considerable confusion. Either way, disillusion is likely to settle upon what might otherwise have been a very worthwhile institution.

In other management or planning teams members may all be expected to operate at the same broad work level (see Figure 6.3). Cross-departmental coordinating committees are of such a kind; so are many project groups or working parties; so too sometimes are top-management bodies in local government or health services, at least as they currently exist in Britain (see Chapter 11). Here, a more senior person, B1, may well take the chair and generally act as leader. But suitable procedures for such groups are quite different than for the

Figure 6.2

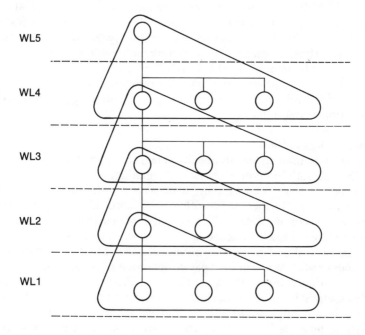

two-tier management teams just discussed. Here, it is quite inappropriate for the leader to overrule any other member on a matter which that particular individual considers of prime importance, let alone a view held by the majority. (Hence, unresolved issues may need to be referred back to a higher authority or authorities.) There may be scope for the exercise of co-ordinating authority (as described in Chapter 2) with instructions to match. But there is no room for a main line-managerial relationship.

Figure 6.3

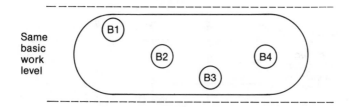

Even more complex structures may arise in the sorts of direct-action teams which bring together professional practitioners and their associates from a variety of different disciplines and agencies – doctors, nurses, social workers and various paramedical staff, for example. Here, people may often be found in posts at several different work levels (commonly level 1, 2 or 3). And a whole range of different authority relationships may need to be recognised among various of the parties involved: main line-managerial, co-ordinating, supervisory, prescribing, and so on.[7]

Matrix Organisation
So far, in examining the multiplicity of real choices behind the facades of 'bureaucratic' or 'non-bureaucratic' organisation we have looked at the specific topics of hierarchy, management style, innovation and teamwork. A further topic often mentioned in this particular discussion is (as indicated in Table 6.1) that of matrix organisation – a subject already briefly touched upon in fact in Chapter 5.

The basic idea of matrix organisation is one in which organisational strands exist in two or more separate dimensions.[8] A common pattern is a two-dimensional matrix (as shown in Figure 6.4) in which one dimension is based on different *functions*, whilst the second is based on different *projects, products, clientele*, or *places*. Alternatively, division by *place* itself may figure as the prime dimension, or some mixture of *place* and *function*.

A structure like this is often depicted as something radically different from the basic hierarchic or bureaucratic pattern. But again, such a broad characterisation is of little practical help when it comes to detailed organisational design. In matrix organisation, as elsewhere, there are specific choices to be made about responsibilities and authority. Leadership of some kind is still needed, and needed moreover in each separate dimension of activity. Who, if anybody, is

Figure 6.4

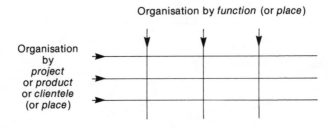

to carry main line-managerial roles (as earlier defined)? Where leading figures in either dimension do not act in such roles, do they nevertheless carry authority of some kind, and if so, exactly what?'

More fundamentally, the fact that a complex organisational form has been adopted does not mean that the question of the expected work level in different jobs disappears or becomes irrelevant. The case where all in a given matrix work at the same level is not an impossible one – it may, for example, be found or approached in academic or professional communities – but it is untypical. Commonly, closer investigation reveals a clear expectation that leaders in one dimension should operate at a higher work level than either those led or leaders in the other dimension.

Consider, for example, the industrial organisation depicted in Figure 6.5, where the main functional departments of marketing, production, and research and development are cross-cut by some product-management system. Exploration in any such case might well show that the functional heads were expected to operate at level 4, all developing and running comprehensive services in their own fields. And it might well show that each in his or her own field carried in practice something close to main line-managerial authority and responsibility, as earlier defined. By contrast, the so-called product managers might well be found to play a monitoring and co-ordinating role, with authority to instruct and review, but not to set new policies, make appraisals of personal performance, change people's jobs, or affect their careers. And it might well be discovered that the activities expected of the latter implied a level 3 rather than a level 4 view – developing systematic approaches in the medium term but not developing comprehensive facilities in the longer term.

Of course, other patterns of work level and authority are possible in these or other settings. But the main point stands. Although matrix organisation is clearly something different from a simple one-

Figure 6.5

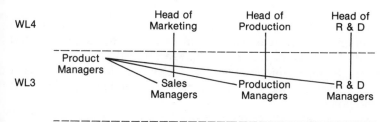

dimensional management system, the underlying hierarchy in the work to be done still remains, and still demands organisational recognition.

Decentralisation

We may now turn to another topic often raised in the context of discussions of so-called bureaucratic or non-bureaucratic organisation: that of decentralisation.

Much play is made in modern management writing on the common need as businesses get beyond a certain size for their transformation to a radically different structure referred to as 'decentralised' or sometimes 'divisionalised'. Reference is often made to the way in which a number of prominent American enterprises like General Motors, Dupont, Standard Oil and Sears Roebuck pioneered this pattern in the expansive era of the 1920s, changing (as Donald Schon later put it) from 'a pyramid built around a single relatively-static product line, to a constellation of semi-autonomous divisions'.[10] Again, a work-levels approach reveals new aspects of the matter and clarifies practical choices.

Often, any shift at all from organisation based on *function* to one based on *product, market* or *territory* is loosely described as 'decentralising' or 'divisionalising'. But this is not really definitive. Divisionalisation or decentralisation in the fullest sense involves the establishment of substantial, self-contained organisational units, each with its own comprehensive terms of reference, and each with its own complete set of financial targets and budgets. Work levels help pinpoint the situation. It is precisely at level 4 and above that such forms come into their own. At level 3, or even lower, it is certainly possible to set up things called divisions, with so-called general managers in charge. However, it can be predicted with confidence that it will not prove realistic for such managers to engage in comprehensive, long-term planning, or to carry their own budgets for staff and capital as well as more fluid resources, or to be held accountable for the creation of profits or financial surpluses. Decentralisation or divisionalisation in the specific sense just described simply will not work at this level or below.

If there is to be reasonable self-containment, any divisionalisation according to particular *function* will (as noted in the last chapter) usually be ruled out. The obvious bases are indeed, therefore, *product, market* (*clientele*), or *territory*. Nevertheless, it is the expected level of work – level 4 or above – which is, as we suggest, really crucial to the conception.

Brief mention may be made at this point of the 'small is beautiful' thesis.[11] This has no doubt acted as a useful counterbalance to the modern obsession with size for its own sake. However, the more discriminating question (absolutely necessary in any serious design approach) is to ask just how big or small any organisation needs to be in relation to its own particular character and purpose. Many clubs, communes and recreational societies, for example, need to stay reasonably small if they are to retain real conviviality. And many local services are best provided by little businesses or partnerships, operating no higher than level 3 and employing no more than a few dozen people. But something bigger is clearly needed if, for example, central government is to continue to function adequately; if comprehensive health, education and welfare services of modern standards are to be provided; if electricity and other power are to be efficiently produced; and if large-scale chemical processing and engineering work are to be carried out. Here, large territories must be comprehensively covered, and planning undertaken which sometimes has to look up to several decades ahead. The required work may be level 4 or 5, even level 6 or 7. In the latter case, tens or even hundreds of thousands of people may need to be employed.

If, in such cases, the benefits of size are to be held on to and the manifest disbenefits avoided, effective decentralisation becomes an issue of paramount importance. In the very largest organisations something more than plain divisionalisation (as it has just been defined) is in fact possible. This is the creation of complete operating subsidiaries, each with full level 5 terms of reference and each with its own separate governing body and legal identity. (In level 7 organisations, these might be grouped into a further layer of level 6 complexes, each again, with its own distinct legal identity.)

To repeat, the level 5 undertaking is a fully developed enterprise of its own; one with the widest possible operational brief; one that should be capable of bringing about its own continuing transformation. Such bodies need not themselves be extremely large. Even the most labour-intensive need employ only a few thousand staff, say ten thousand at the most. Given a separate governing body of some kind (even though ultimately subordinate to some higher holding company or machinery of State), participation in the process of governance by employees becomes a more-realistic possibility (see discussion later in this chapter). So does real public participation and accountability, whether it be exercised through the law courts, through the direct election or appointment of public representatives to the governing bodies concerned, or more indirectly through the impact of the news media or local pressure groups on governing body members. (See further discussion of this general topic in Chapters 10 and 11.)

Enhancing Employee Participation

Exploring one by one the various topics listed at the start of the chapter, we come finally to the subject of participation, or, more specifically, the possibilities of enhanced participation for the employees themselves, in large organisations.

The flow of history would certainly suggest room for many practical improvements in this particular area. Since the start of the century, under the impact of Taylorism and Scientific Management, it has been the fate of countless workers to have their jobs systematically method-studied, timed, prescribed and deskilled. 'Remove all possible brainwork from the shop' was Taylor's own original cry. Whatever the gain in crude productivity, the price that has been paid in terms of boredom, alienation and dehumanisation is huge (as Henry Braverman has so vividly brought to notice[12]).

The reaction started around the 1950s, with the first experiments in deliberate job enlargement in IBM. As time went on, prompted much by Frederick Herzberg, the idea developed not simply of enlarging jobs – adding one Mickey Mouse task to another, in the graphic phrase – but of enriching them by the deliberate addition of work of greater responsibility and complexity.[13] In firms like Volvo, Saab-Scania and Philips, small gangs of workers were given collective responsibility for some complete assembly task. Eventually, the 'quality of working life movement' (as it began to be described) was seen as encompassing not only job enlargement, job enrichment and autonomous work-groups, but a whole range of broader experiments in worker participation. These included co-determinition schemes like the ones adopted in the iron and steel industries of West Germany after the Second World War in which 'worker directors' sat on governing boards; all manner of consultative committees and works councils; and full-scale experiments in worker ownership and control as in the Israeli kibbutzim (starting from the 1920s), the post-war Yugoslavian factories, and the celebrated producer co-operatives of Mondragón in Northern Spain.

All in all, much significant experimentation and development has occurred in this field. Many real departures have been made from established ways. But in certain respects things have remained resolutely unchanged. The evidence points clearly to the fact that, in practice, hierarchy always seems to survive in some form or another.[14] Neither full control by workers or overall policy and direction (as in the Yugoslavian or Mondragón factories) nor the sharing in such (as in German and other co-determination schemes) negates the need for some effective chain of executive management. The different levels of work are always there.

In practice, most job-enlargement or job-enrichment schemes have been in effect about increasing the content or discretion in level 1 factory jobs, whilst still leaving them within some framework of clear output prescription. The existence of a number of top level 1 supervisory or inspectorial posts may thereby have been undermined, but the need for superstructures of managerial jobs at level 2 and beyond has still remained. Even where full-scale autonomous work groups have been established, they have usually been, it seems, autonomous only in matters of the division and sequencing of particular sub-tasks. Their activities have still been constrained within a prescribed output package (the specification of the particular automobile or TV set required or whatever), decided by planners and managers at higher levels.

Using the ideas developed in this book a new view is revealed of what is, and is not, realistic in the promotion of greater participation by workers. For a start it must be assumed that those in a typical cross-section of the population will never show equal capability for any given level of managerial or executive work (any more than they will show equal capability at butchery, baking or candlestick-making). This means that, in striving for greater participation, it can never be a realistic goal to try and arrange things so that everybody is equally involved in activity at every level, either simultaneously or in rotation. (Not, that is, with typical cross-sections of the population; with atypical groupings, where for one reason or another members can be expected to be much closer in level-of-work ability, things may be rather different.) The task must be to establish a system which makes the maximum use of people's different level-of-work abilities as they exist at any given time, some high, some middle, some low; a system, moreover, which is continuously sensitive to the way in which the ability of each individual changes and develops as time goes by. (And here, of course, is where the key role of the main line-manager comes in.) This is surely the first and most direct way of enhancing participation. It is by using to the full all such abilities as each individual may have in the main job which each carries out; or to put it another way, by scrupulously avoiding underemployment, temporary or permanent.

But other important possibilities do exist. For a start, there is a strong case over and beyond seeing that all are fully-employed in their prime jobs, for involving them to some degree in executive work at higher levels as well. It is highly desirable for level 1 workers to meet regularly with their level 2 bosses (not just with top-level 1 supervisors) in various quality circles, productivity committees, section meetings and the like. It will be a good thing for level 2 people to join with their level 3 bosses in various management teams of the kind described earlier in the chapter; level 3 people with their level 4 bosses; and so on. All such things will be particularly beneficial for those who, in terms of their own personal capabilities, are well on the way to the next work level. But it will be by no means unimportant for others who are well able to contribute useful information, ideas, criticism or proposals, even though they themselves may never develop the ability to make good final judgements in the matters concerned.

It is predictable, however, that what will not work are teams concerned with executive decision-making which span more than two work levels. Exceptional individuals apart, those from the bottom rung will simply not comprehend the scope and range of executive issues being faced by those at the topmost rung. They will in consequence often feel out of their depth or belittled. By contrast, those from the top level will often feel held back or anchored down by the very narrow and concrete way in which those from the bottom level are perceiving things. Far from enhancing participation, such experiences are more likely to discredit it.

Does this mean that there is no scope at all for groups, meetings, or discussions which cross a large number of work levels? We do not suggest so for a moment. We have been at pains throughout to emphasize that work levels apply to *executive* activity, in its broadest sense. Policy-making and the fixing of general rules, procedures, and entitlements – what might in equally broad terms be described as *governance* –is quite another thing. There are strong arguments for allowing workers at all levels to participate in some way in the governance of the enterprise as a whole. Possible mechanisms include surveys and referenda, open meetings, works councils, consultative committees, and worker representatives on governing bodies. (Which of these works best is another discussion.) Such a mode of part-icipation, crossing, as we say, many different work levels, may have a potent effect on morale and corporate well-being. All cannot hope to be equally gifted executants. But all in this way may be helped to share in a sense of common citizenship.

To sum up, then, the first thing that the approach which we have developed stresses, is not just the desirability of job enrichment for factory workers or other designated categories, but something much more radical: the necessity for all in employment of whatever sort, to have work of a level which is well matched to their own individual and changing abilities. (For many, this might mean jobs of significantly higher level, but for some, of course, it could mean jobs of lower level.) As regards the general governance of the enterprise, there appears to be no bar (putting it at its most neutral) to the development of machinery which cuts across many levels. As regards executive activity, there appear to be good possibilities for people regularly participating in decision-making at the next work level above that of their main job, but not beyond. Resulting patterns of participation over and above that of being employed to the full in one's prime job are thus as shown in Figure 6.6.

Figure 6.6 Possible avenues of employee participation

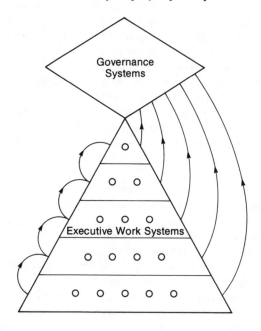

Conclusion

In Chapter 5 a series of prime design decisions were considered. It was suggested that, until these were properly settled, no others could be satisfactorily dealt with. But many other organisational issues there certainly are.

In this chapter we have tackled head-on the notion that the design approach might apply to the issues of so-called bureaucratic organisation but not to those of other alternative or more advanced types. We have emphasised that differences in work level arise in organisations of all types, bureaucratic or non-bureaucratic, autocratic or democratic, public or private, capitalist or communist.

And we have emphasised that so, too, do various issues of structural authority (which is to be distinguished from managerial style).

The fact is that descriptions such as 'bureaucratic' and 'non-bureaucratic' are really stereotypes (or, to use the rather more respectful language of sociologists, 'ideal types'). They do not provide any specific models or options for action. One could never in practice introduce, as described and *en bloc*, a non-bureaucratic structure to replace some pre-existing bureaucratic one, let alone carry out the reverse process. The identification of broad types such as these may alert one to general directions of change. But practical change itself has to be instituted through innumerable small and specific steps: introducing or repealing written job descriptions; revising departmental structures; setting up new teams or committees; bringing in new methods of participation; introducing new systems of planning, budgeting and delegation; introducing new arrangements for pay and career progression; and so on and so forth. In respect of some of these matters changes that appear more or less 'non-bureaucratic' may be preferred; for others, changes or clarifications that appear more or less 'bureaucratic'. And – we return to the main point – in the first type of practical change as in the second, considerations of work levels and authority relationships will be equally germane.

In this chapter we have looked in fact at some of the practical issues in specifying required levels of innovation. We have looked at some of the practical issues in teamwork, matrix organisation, and decentralisation. We have looked at some of the practical issues in attempts of various kinds to enhance employee participation. We do not pretend that the discussion of any of these topics has been fully comprehensive. Nor do we suggest that these, even together with the other issues considered in earlier chapters, exhaust the list of all that may arise in a complex organisation. The overall aim has been to indicate something of the general range of issues to which work-level ideas and others offered here may be applied. With this done, the task of Part One, the statement of the design approach in general terms, is complete. In Part Two we shall proceed to describe how the approach applies in practice in a variety of more specific fields and settings.

Notes

1. Leading statements are to be found in D. McGregor, *The Human Side of Enterprise*, New York, McGraw Hill, 1960; T. Burns, and G. M. Stalker, *The Management of Innovation*, London, Tavistock, 1961; H. Mintzberg, *The Structuring of Organisation*, Englewood Cliffs, NJ, Prentice Hall, 1979.

2. See P. R. Lawrence and J. W. Lorsch, *Organisation and Environment*, Boston, Harvard University Press, 1967.

3. See McGregor, *The Human Side of Enterprise*.

4. T. J. Peters and R. H. Waterman, *In Search of Excellence: Lessons from America's Best-Run Companies*, New York, Harper & Row, 1982. The long list of other writers on organisation who have talked primarily about style or culture rather than structure includes such figures as Elton Mayo, Kurt Lewin, Chris Argyris, Rensis Likert, Daniel Katz, Warren Bennis, Edgar Schein and Robert Blake.

5. See Burns and Stalker, *The Management of Innovation*. See also F. E. Emery and E. L. Trist, 'The Causal Texture of Organizational Environments' in F. E. Emery, ed., *Systems Thinking*, Harmondsworth, Penguin, 1969.

6. An idea promoted many years ago by Rensis Likert in his book *New Patterns of Management*, New York, McGraw Hill, 1961.

7. See E. Jaques, ed., *Health Services*, London, Heinemann, 1978, Chapter 10.

8. See S. M. Davies and P. R. Lawrence, *Matrix*, Reading, MA, Addison-Wesley, 1977; and K. Knight, ed., *Matrix Management*, Farnborough, Hants, Gower, 1977.

9. See discussions in Knight, *Matrix Management*.

10. D.A. Schon, *Beyond the Stable State*, London, Temple Smith, 1971, Chapter 3.

11. E.F. Schumacher, *Small is Beautiful*, London, Abacus, 1974.

12. See H. Braverman, *Labour and Monopoly Capital*, New York, Monthly Review Press, 1974.

13. See F. Herzberg, *Work and the Nature of Man*, London, Staples Press, 1968.

14. See A. S. Tannenbaum, *et al.*, *Hierarchy in Organisation*, London, Jossey Bass, 1974.

PART TWO
SPECIFIC
APPLICATIONS

7 Factory Organisation

In this second part of the book we describe how the general design approach discussed in Part One has been applied and developed in a variety of specific fields and settings as opportunities to do so have naturally arisen over the past fifteen to twenty years. In later chapters we look at applications to front-line selling and service work; to the organisation of professionals in public services; to top structures in industry and commerce; and to top structures in health services and local government.

In this chapter we concentrate on questions of factory organisation (using the phrase to encompass production plants of all kinds). In doing so we draw upon consultancy and training work in four large industrial corporations in the fields of engineering, household appliances, chemicals and metal-processing. And we also draw upon a number of discussions in workshops at Brunel University with managers from a further variety of production fields, including pharmaceuticals, shoe-production, paper-production, and nuclear-fuel processing.

All these discussions, the shorter as well as the longer, have provided positive opportunities to test the validity of the design approach described in earlier chapters to the organisational problem of particular factories. Certain issues have regularly emerged. Although somewhat varied in kind, and not together offering any comprehensive list, they nevertheless appear to be of general interest and concern. They are as follows:

- the ambiguous role of the foreman;
- confusion about the relative tasks and responsibilities of higher managers (superintendents, works managers, factory managers, production directors, and so on);
- difficulties of integrating specialist staff and line management;
- difficulties of getting satisfactory career paths both for pro-

fessional staff and for those who have risen from the shop floor;
* uncertainty about managerial responsibilities in shift work.

Let us look at each in more detail, showing how the ideas of different authority relationships, work levels, and ability levels elucidate each and help expose practical options.

Clarifying the Role of the Foreman

Perhaps the most striking and consistent issue to emerge from the work described is the highly ambiguous role of the foreman. In one of the factories, for example, the foreman supposedly allocated and controlled labour. But recently instituted scheduling sections had taken over most of these functions. In fact, in the words of one manager of the company, 'foremen do as they are damned well told'. Union officials in the same company declared that the existing job description for foremen was in their view quite worthless.

Generally amongst production managers we have found great doubt as to whether foremen are really part of 'us' or 'them': junior members of the management team, or leading hands with the basic work-force. Foremen are often described as, and encouraged to think of themselves as, 'first-line management'. But they seldom seem to be granted much real authority or status, Moreover, being directly promoted from the shop floor, they naturally tend to be seen as, and see themselves as, in a different category from other members of management, many of whom will never have worked in regular shop-floor jobs and most of whom (nowadays) will have gone through some extensive process of college education.

The crucial question is this: is the foreman expected to act as the first main line-manager at work level 2, or as a supervisor at the top of level 1?

If genuinely conceived as a main line-manager (as defined in Chapter 2) any foreman should have a right of say, at minimum a veto, in all appointments of staff under his control. And he should have a right to make significant alterations in individual responsibilities or to initiate changes in pay or grade, or (in the extreme) to initiate transfer or dismissal, according to his own judgement about how each performs in practice. If in a genuine level 2 post, any foreman would, by definition, be expected to make or shape his own personal responses to open-ended situations facing him, albeit always within some given framework or system set by higher management. Such 'open-ended situations' might arise from problems with individual personnel, from complex technical issues, shortage of materials, sudden changes of priorities, emergencies, breakdowns and so on. The resulting post might perhaps be better titled 'section manager'[1] rather than just 'foreman'.

By contrast, foremen conceived as top-level 1 supervisors should *not* have powers at their own discretion to veto new appointments, make significant alterations to general responsibilities, take official steps to change pay or grade, or to initiate transfer or dismissal. They might well be encouraged to express views on these things. But decisions and actions should rest with the level 2 managers, whoever they are. The essential role of foremen thus viewed, would be to help level 2 managers in charge of large numbers of subordinates by doing things like allocating individual jobs, maintaining the necessary supply of materials and tools, arranging repairs to machines, sorting out minor technical problems, inducting new staff, and checking on discipline. Given an expectation of work limited to level 1, it ought to be possible, in principle at least, to furnish clear guides as to the desirable outcomes for any situations which are likely to be faced – or to indicate where referral to the manager at level 2 was necessary. In other words, it ought to be possible to give precise answers to all questions of the kind 'what should I do if. . .'? This does not mean that no discretion would be called for. On the contrary, such top-level 1 supervisory posts would demand people who could draw as appropriate upon substantial practical experience in the setting concerned, and handle personal relationships to good effect.

As we say, the typical foreman role often hovers uncertainly (and somewhat ineffectually) between these two models: the full-scale level 2 manager and the top-level 1 supervisor. In fact, separate posts of both kinds are usually called for. There will always be the need if there is to be strong management, to identify who carries (under whatever title) the main burden of level 2 responsibilities. But each such level 2 manager, particularly in labour-intensive industry, will commonly need the support of one or more top-level 1 supervisors.

In establishing and differentiating these two kinds of job it will usually be a mistake to reclassify all existing foremen, *en bloc*, as level 2 section managers, or all existing charge-hands (or whatever more junior grades already exist) as level 1 supervisors. A much more careful appraisal of individual ability is called for. Taking the first line, many individuals could well find themselves in jobs that they were simply not up to; taking the second, others could find their real abilities seriously underused. Selectivity in individual appointment would be the key to any effective change. (Particular care would be needed in the handling of staff currently only capable of working with full confidence at level 1, but judged likely to be ready for level 2 responsibility in a few years' time.)

Clarifying Higher Factory Management

One of the other more striking things to emerge from the work described has been the number and confusion of management posts often evident in the line above foremen. It appears impossible to assume with confidence anything about the real powers and responsibilities of management posts from name alone. Titles seem more or less interchangeable and with no very dependable indications of relative status: superintendents, shop managers, production managers, works managers, general works managers, factory managers, production directors, technical directors, manufacturing directors, directors of operations, and so on.

Levels often proliferate. One factory employing about 2,000 people in the production of metal sheeting had, according to the official chart, no less than five tiers of management above the foreman, namely: supervisor, superintendent, production manager, director of operations, and managing director (of the plant). Three or four levels above foreman seems not uncommon even in smaller plants, not to speak of additional distinctions between general foremen, foremen, charge hands, setters and the like. It was no surprise perhaps that some of the first things complained about in many discussions were the poor communications up and down the line; uncertainty about responsibilities; the need to identify 'key managers', and so on.

Again, the simplest way to cut through any muddle or duplication in this area is to go straight for questions about necessary work levels. As described in Chapter 5, the prime questions are, first, what is the basic expected work level in the plant concerned, the second, what is the highest expected work level? Usually in production work the answer to the first question will be level 1. The answer to the second question – highest expected work-level – could be anything from level 2 to level 4 (the reality or desirability of Level 5 briefs in production work is critically reviewed in Chapter 10). Settling these two questions then determines of course, just how many main management levels are desirable in all (for example two, if the highest expected work is level 3; and three, if the highest expected work is level 4, assuming basic expected work at level 1 in both cases).

We have already looked at the need to establish strong 'section manager' posts at level 2. Any in main management posts at level 3 may be generically described as 'unit managers'.[2] The essential job at this particular level must be to develop and maintain, within given resources of manpower, equipment and buildings, a system capable of responding to any likely flow of orders for the particular products at issue. This involves the development of all sorts of methods and procedures – procedures for handling personnel problems, technical methods, scheduling systems, ordering systems, and so on. Each level 3 unit manager must be expected to be an effective master of the various technologies employed in his or her own area. To avoid over-crowding of management levels, all section managers at level 2 should be directly accountable to appropriate unit managers at level 3, and all unit managers directly accountable to managers at level 4.

Those at level 4 might have any variety of titles. Often at this level the epithet 'general' or 'director' becomes appropriate, as in 'general works manager' or 'production director' (this is the lowest level at which managers could be useful members of corporate boards). The essential job at this level must be the development and maintenance of a comprehensive production facility to handle expected sales in coming years of both existing products and those in course of design or development. In addition to seeing that appropriate systems are being established by managers at the next level down, level 4 production managers should themselves be heavily involved in devising comprehensive plans both for continuing operations and for capital development; working in both cases in close conjunction with colleagues in research, product development, and marketing.

A final note may be added on the title 'factory manager'. From what has already been said it becomes clear – assuming that this title simply means the topmost post in any given plant, large or small – that it can apply to work at a variety of different levels. Often it may stand for a clear level 3 post. But on some occasions it can refer to a level 4 post of 'general manager' or 'production director' status. And in other circumstances again it can refer to a level 2 post equivalent to no more than a 'section manager' job elsewhere.

Integrating Specialist Staff and Line-Management

Another fundamental problem which has emerged in many of our discussions of factory organisation is that of getting a better integra-tion between the work of specialist staff and line managers. All too often we have heard the complaint of 'too much management by specialists' added to that of weak line-management, particularly at lower levels.

In two cases which we came across, the companies concerned were both actively considering ways of delegating responsibility for output, quality and costs further down the line, with appropriate decentral-isation of specialist staff and strengthening of line-management. In the first (a factory of some 1,800 people manufacturing domestic products), the possibility was under consideration of creating a number of separate 'units', each responsible for its own products, and each with its own facilities for methods, minor product-development work, material control, and so forth. In the second (a factory of about the same number of people making mining equipment), there were proposals to establish four 'cells', each (again) responsible for its own product range and each with its own supplies, progress, inspection and maintenance facilities. In both these cases most of the main specialist functions – production engineering, work study, quality control, planning and scheduling, materials procurement, personnel work and cost accounting – were at the time concerned (prior to any reorganisation) located in separate departments whose heads reported very high up in the management chain; in some instances even beyond the top factory post itself. Given such a situation, compounded in both cases with confused line structures, it was not difficult to see why the need for some radical reform was felt.

In going further into this question of where, and how best, to build in specialist functions, the first necessity is in fact to examine the main line-management structure itself. As discussed in Chapter 5, *if the main line-management structure is weak, no amount of fiddling with specialist and supporting posts will ever get things right.* And the key to a sound line structure is, as we suggest, having the right number of posts, each with a full range of 'main line-managerial' authority, just one in each consecutive work level.

With a clear structure of section manager posts at level 2, of unit manager posts at level 3, and of general production manager posts (of whatever title) at level 4, appropriate specialist and support structure can readily be added. Keeping to the principle of an optimum gap of one work level between managers and all their subordinates, specialist or other, the following possibilities emerge in broad outline.

At level 2, besides top-level 1 supervisors of the sort described earlier, section managers may need a few clerical staff or the like to help them, also in level 1 posts. At level 3, given the responsibility for total system maintenance and development, it will usually be necessary for unit managers to have a rather more elaborate range of support staff. In technically advanced units they may need their own engineering, quality control or maintenance specialists. In units with complex scheduling problems they may need a planning specialist. In units with large numbers of staff or difficult industrial relations they may need their own personnel specialist. All such specialist posts would be appropriately pitched at level 2, and in some cases their occupants might themselves need to be supported by subordinate staff at level 1. The provision of such a range of support to level 3 production managers starts to give substance to the idea of the self-contained 'cell' or 'unit' which takes responsibility for its own methods development, quality control, scheduling, and so on.

Figure 7.1

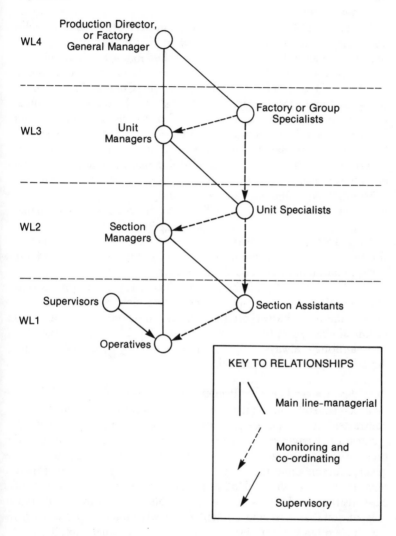

Giving specialist support to main line-managers at level 3 does not, however, mean that main line-managers at level 4 do not also need it. In any large factory, or group of medium-sized ones, there will probably be need, for example, for a personnel specialist at level 3 to take an overall, systematic view of personnel and industrial relations policies. There may well be need for some overall production planner, and for one or more technical specialists also working at this systematic level.

Taking levels 4 and below together, a pattern of line and specialist posts might thus result as illustrated in Figure 7.1. Even with the proper one-level separation of main line-managers and all subordinates, there are clearly some complex relationships to be sorted out here. 'Dual influence' (as described in Chapter 2) has to be recognised and accepted. Relationships shown by the various dotted lines can neither be denied nor written off as 'purely advisory'. It might well be that specialists at one tier (unit specialists for example) should be recognised as playing some sort of 'staff-officer' role of the type described in Chapter 5, in relation to line managers at the next tier down (section managers for example). As such, they would exercise substantial co-ordinating and monitoring authority in their own particular fields, within broad policies and directions set by the higher line-managers (in this case, the unit managers).

As regards relationships between specialists in the same field at two successive tiers (for example factory or group specialists and the corresponding unit specialists), given their one work level separation, it would be strange if the former did not have a say in the appointment of the latter, or in the appraisal of their subsequent performance, or in their training or career progression. It would be strange if many technical changes in the field were not initiated directly between the two, although always, appropriately, within general policies and directions agreed by the main line-managers.

Providing Career Paths for Professional and Shop-Floor Staff

Another general issue that has emerged from our discussions is the contrasted career paths of staff with professional qualifications (professional engineers, college-trained managers and so on), and those who have risen from the shop floor (charge-hands, foremen, general foremen and the like). In some ways this mirrors the classic separation of 'officers' and 'other ranks', with its inevitable flavour of class distinction. There is the specific problem of how to provide first jobs of suitable level and content for newly-qualified professionals who have often had very little previous practical experience. There is also the problem of how to provide suitable jobs for staff who, having risen from the shop floor, reveal potential for further development.

Two things can help. The first is the recognition that the crucial thing is not social background or even formal qualification, but the actual ability levels of different individuals and their different rates of maturation. The second is (again) the existence of a sound management structure, and in particular, a proper separation of level 2 section-manager posts from top-level 1 supervisory posts.

Given such a backgrond it is not difficult to spell out the main possibilities (see Figure 7.2). As regards section-manager posts themselves, there is no reason why they should not be filled either by professionals or by ex-shop-floor staff, provided that the individuals in question are of clear level 2 ability. Below this level, however, some differentiation may be needed. For many shop-floor staff on their way up, a top-level 1 supervisory post may provide the obvious stepping-stone. (Some indeed, may stop here, the leap to level 2 always beyond them.) On the other hand, the basic supposition for professionally qualified staff is that they are going to move rapidly into level 2 jobs. Any role with a clear level 1 content, even a top-level 1 supervisory role, may be quite unsuitable for them, once qualified. But they may well at first lack the confidence and experience to leap directly to management responsibilities at level 2. For them, the first appropriate stage may be some sort of assistant-manager job, a job with plenty of scope to test out emerging 'situational response' capabilities, but with frequent supervision and close support at hand when confidence fails. After a year or so – less in some cases – they may be ready to assume full level 2 responsibilities either in line-management or in some supporting or specialist job.

For staff from the shop floor who turn out as time goes on to be capable of levels of work beyond section manager (that is for work at

Figure 7.2 Possible career paths for upward-moving shop-floor and professional staff

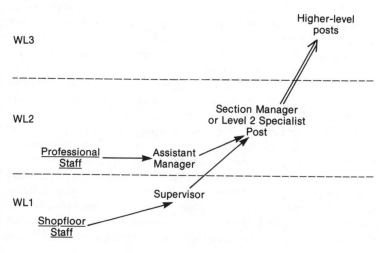

level 3 or above) no special structure of posts would appear to be necessary. What may well be needed is the time and opportunity for them to undertake some significant management or professional training at a later point in their career. But this is a different thing.

Defining Managerial Responsibilities in Shift Work

The final issue of general interest to arise from our various discussions is that of responsibilities in shift work. In one particular plant in which metal sheeting was processed on a continuous twenty-four-hour cycle, this issue was sharply posed in the form of the question 'who is responsible when things go wrong at three o'clock in the morning?'. Was it (in this particular case) the shift foreman on duty, the superintendent at home in bed, the production manager in charge of the whole factory, or who?

In a general way, all in any line of command must of course carry some responsibility for whatever happens. The real questions here are (a) what particular matters managers at each level should be held personally and directly responsible for dealing with, and (b) in consequence, just what level of manager needs to be physically on call or on duty at any time.

As regards the first question, managers at level 2 – section managers for example, in production work – are by definition the people who are supposed to be dealing with the bulk of concrete problems, or drawing them to the attention of their superiors where, in the minority of cases, they cannot. If bad judgements are made in specific instances it is their direct responsibility (unless they have referred the matter up). But they are not responsible for setting the general systems. This next layer of responsibility rests with level 3 managers – unit managers or the like in production work. If the systems are bad it is these latter who are prima facie to blame. If the failure is due to some absolute lack of provision of necessary facilities it is the level 4 managers who are prima facie to blame. And so on.

Proceeding, then, to the question of who needs to be on duty or on call, there is normally in any twenty-four-hour operation one particular shift during daytime when higher-level managers are mostly present. At other times it would usually appear necessary to have staff present in any given plant who are capable of, and have the necessary authority and experience to cope with, open-ended problem situations; that is, to act decisively at level 2. There might conceivably be cases where top-level 1 supervision was all that was required. But in any event it would certainly not appear necessary to have staff beyond level 2 actually on duty. More senior managers may need to be on call, but sustained work at level 3 or higher is not required. Whole systems do not need to be changed at three o'clock in the morning; nor does the total range of provision. (Both kinds of change, any case, usually take weeks, months or even years to institute.)

This conclusion – of the need in shift work for staff of no higher than level 2 capability to be directly physically available – would seem to be a general one. It would appear to apply not only to continuous production units but to other twenty-four-hour operating plants like hospitals, police stations or airports.

Summary

Work levels and other ideas in the general design approach described earlier throw new light on a number of typical issues in factory organisation. They help to cut through the marked ambiguity in the typical foreman role – an ambiguity which can cause fatal weakness in many production systems at one of the most critical points. They suggest the need for a clear separation of level 2 section managers and top-level 1 supervisors. And at higher levels, they indicate the need for a clear separation of level 3 unit managers (concerned primarily with developing and maintaining specific systems) and level 4 general managers (concerned primarily with developing and maintaining comprehensive production facilities).

Given a strong and uncluttered central management line, it becomes much easier to build in support and specialist staff. In particular it becomes possible, within larger factories, to develop separate level 3 units with the sort of specialist staff to enable them to cope, to a large extent, with their own quality control, scheduling, technical and personnel issues.

The general approach also suggests how invidious distinctions can be reduced between college-educated managers and those who have risen from the shop floor, and how better career paths can be developed for both. And it offers concrete proposals for appropriate assignment of management responsibilities in shift work.

Notes

1. The term 'section manager' used in this particular way is taken from the Glacier Project, as is the term 'unit manager' used later in the chapter. Most of the issues discussed in this chapter were explored in earlier years in a major development project in the Glacier Metal Company, in which the importance of a proper definition of main line-management roles and their correct vertical separation became appreciated at an early point (although without the aid of the specific work-level descriptions offered in this book). See W. Brown *Exploration in Management*, London, Heinemann, 1960.
2. The term 'unit manager', as used here, is also taken from the Glacier Project.

8 Selling and Service Work

In this chapter we continue our description of how the general design approach applies in particular fields by looking at a miscellany of activities all broadly describable as selling and service work. In doing so we draw on discussions of current problems with relevant managers attending our Brunel workshops and consultancy and research work in a variety of service-giving organisations, public, private and voluntary. Specifically we shall look at:

- front-line jobs in commerce (salesmen, bank clerks, and so on);
- front-line jobs in welfare (home helps, care attendants, and so on);
- personnel and training jobs;
- research and development jobs;
- secretarial jobs;
- administrative and managerial jobs.

The common problem that threads together this rather heterogeneous list is the considerable ambiguity often evident as regards work level. Such ambiguity has significant and debilitating consequences. It bedevils recuitment and selection. It makes realistic appraisal of performance impossible. It means many people in the wrong jobs: some trying desperately to master work which is in fact beyond them; others more or less painfully aware that the tasks actually demanded of them are not putting their energies and abilities to anything like full enough use. Above all, it frequently produces major uncertainties at crucial points of service delivery. In the case of later items in the list it is a question of the intermediate delivery of services within the organisation – not so serious perhaps. In the case of the first two items however, it is a question of the final delivery of goods of services to individual customers or clients.

Let us consider each of the areas listed above in turn.

Front-Line Jobs in Commerce

We have come across various examples among what might be described as front-line jobs in commerce – in selling, banking, insurance, building societies, travel agencies, airlines, and so on – where there appears to be considerable confusion as to whether level 1 or level 2 work is really required. All these jobs are white-collar, and universally regarded as of higher status than blue-collar or manual ones. They are usually salaried rather than hourly paid, and are frequently accompanied by good perquisites and attractive working conditions. Since they involve direct and regular interaction with customers, those who fill them must be of acceptable personality and appearance. For all these reasons such jobs often attract people of some intelligence and ability. Even if specific professional training is not necessary, those with good general educational qualifications are often preferred when it comes to selection. In certain cases a direct attempt is made to employ only university graduates or the equivalent. Very often in fact the tendency, recognised or not, is to recruit people who are either of already existent level 2 ability, or are well on the way to developing such ability.

But do the jobs concerned always provide work at this same level? The answer in many cases must be an unequivocal no. With the widespread advent of computers, much basic work in areas like banking, insurance, or retail selling, has to be absolutely tied down as regards ends or outcomes, even if some degree of freedom is left as regards ways or means. In past years, the typical clerk or salesman might have been allowed some discretion on whether, for example, to put the customer through a check on credit worthiness, or freedom to decide what precise terms of sale or service to offer. Now, the diligent systems analyst will have made amply sure that such slackness or uncertainty (as it appears from his point of view) has been totally removed. In other words, much of this work is now located firmly and permanently with level 1.

However, this will not be universally the case. The point of a work-level analysis is not to fix once and for all the significance of any given job title or occupational group. It is to draw attention to ambiguities and options and to identify possible cases where differences are actually called for.

The title 'salesman' or 'salesperson' for example, can legitimately be applied to jobs at several different work levels. The great bulk of sales staff who work in retail shops or stores may very well nowadays be required to operate no higher than level 1. However, it is different where sales people have to travel widely, to meet customers on their own ground, and to deal rapidly with queries and problems. Here, the basic expectation is often at level 2. Within the limits of given marketing and pricing policies, the typical travelling sales representative will often be expected to exercise some degree of discretion on the best reponse to the particular needs of each particular customer. The shape of the final 'contract' may be left somewhat open-ended. There may be judgements to be made on appropriate discounts; on what degree of deviations from standard product specifications to accept; on what exact delivery dates to promise, on what goods to agree to take back, in view of say, claimed substandard quality, or straightforward over-stocking.

There are other cases again, where a more complex product or service is on offer, and where relationships with customers require meticulous development over long periods of time. Here, the job of the representative may even rise to level 3. Examples are the representative of a computer firm who is selling not just standard hardware or programmes, but complex systems which have to be carefully interwoven with the customer's specific requirements as they are progressively introduced. Another is the seller of insurance or investment packages which have again to be designed specifically to fit in with the customer's own special, and again quite complex, arrangements.[1]

Occasionally, then, front-line commercial jobs may be pitched as high as level 3. More often they will be pitched at either level 1 or level 2. In the end it must depend on exactly what sort of service it is required to provide to individual customers and what sort of immediate response to offer to their needs (a choice likely to have crucial effects on long-term business success or failure).

As regards the kind of people recruited, where the jobs really are level 2, there are no doubt many cases where misguided but consistent efforts are made to fill them with people of level 1 ability. Our own observations suggest, however, that the problem is frequently the other way round. As was suggested earlier, there seems to be a widespread tendency in this particular area to recruit people of level 2 ability for jobs which are, in spite of outward appearances, based firmly in level 1. In such instances the occasional individual, particularly in small organisations, achieves a triumph over the system by somehow contriving to create space in which to use his or her personal abilities to the full (whether or not managing at the same time to get a level of pay commensurate with the real responsibilities taken on). More often this does not happen, so that large numbers of people are left grossly underemployed. This is a situation which promotes neither productivity nor happiness. Predictably, as boredom and frustration rise, so will staff turnover, clock-watching, and absence from work.

Front-Line Jobs in Welfare Work

From our extensive research and consultancy in welfare agencies, both statutory and voluntary, it is evident that widespread ambiguity exists as regards expected work in many front-line jobs in these fields, too. We shall leave until the next chapter a discussion of the situation of professionally-qualified staff (where ambiguity about the basic work level is not usually the main problem) and look for the moment at the numerous unqualified employees and volunteers who undertake direct work with clients – the care attendants, home helps, welfare aides, visitors, meals deliverers, drivers, and so on.

Here is another area where uncertainty about levels is rife. Over the years we have heard many expressions of resentment from people who find in practice that they are being asked to tackle essentially the same tasks as their professionally qualified colleagues, though paid at much lower levels (if paid at all). We have heard some who go on, nevertheless, to express a sense of their own basic capabilities to rise to such demands. We have heard others again who obviously feel out of their depth, and in sore need of closer support and guidance.

Which of these front-line jobs really are suited to unqualified people of average or everyday talents, and which call for the higher level of ability usually associated with professional work? Which of those who currently carry out these jobs are basically capable of the higher level of work even if they need vocational training of some kind, and which are not and may never be, regardless of how carefully they are prepared for it?

Again, a work-level analysis allows the issues and options to be seen more clearly. Again, the correct starting point must be exactly what sort of output is required at the front line; exactly what sort of response is desired to meet the needs of individual clients. There are without doubt many jobs in the welfare field which can be satisfactorily defined in level 1 terms. Delivering food, transporting a child or frail person to hospital or day centre, cleaning somebody's home, helping them to dress, wash and eat; all these activities can often be given a clear prescribed output or end-point as far as is practically significant, and all can thus be held somewhere in the level 1 range. There are other jobs, however, in which it may be difficult or inappropriate to try to pin down the exact end-products required: such things as visiting people's homes to make a general check on their physical and social well-being; providing practical assistance in the home to whole families in difficulty; looking after particularly demanding categories of people in care (disturbed children or mentally ill adults being rehabilitated in the community, for example). Here, a level 2 specification may be more fitting.

There are two reasons for making a firm choice about which level of work really is required in any such case. Firstly, as we stress, it is highly desirable to be clear what one is really trying to achieve with clientele. Is it really possible to judge the needs of various categories of client sufficiently well beforehand, so that a 'prescribed output' service can be defined and delivered? Or is an open-ended appraisal of the needs of each individual client essential at some point or other in the proceedings? Is the basic expected work level 1 or level 2? If the latter, is it level 2 but with the possibility or regular delegation of specific tasks to auxiliaries working at level 1?

Secondly, the choice of expected work level has major implications (again) – for recuitment and training. Jobs at level 2 are best filled by those of commensurate ability; people of only level 1 ability will find them impossible. Likewise, jobs at level 1 are best filled by people of level 1 capability; those of higher ability will find them constraining and frustrating. However, if a basic ability to operate at level 2 is present in the worker concerned, even if it has not been refined and sharpened by specific professional training (and regardless of pay) then it will manifest itself given half a chance.

Following this last point, our sense sometimes is of front-line welfare jobs allowed in practice to drift up into level 2 in response to the worker's own manifest abilities (whether or not this is in the best interest of the overall service). But not all jobs can move in this way. There must be many thousands of middle-aged women currently employed in unqualified or voluntary welfare work, whose career and formal education has been hindered by marriage or child-rearing, who are in fact capable of 'situational response' work. Often their current jobs offer only a partial opportunity to use their full abilities, sometimes not even that. This would seem a prodigal waste of valuable talent.

Another good example of ambiguity in expected work levels in the welfare field is provided by the situation of the typical social security clerk in present-day Britain. On the face of things the aim is to provide a system in which the rights of every applicant for benefit are absolutely clear-cut. And, if the outcome in any given circumstance is predeterminable, the work of processing applications ought (by definition) to be level 1. In fact, the 'rule book' has swollen to such proportions as complex regulation has followed complex regulation that it has become by all accounts well-nigh impossible even to find a way through it, let alone to provide an unequivocal answer to each case presented. More and more, it would seem, local staff are forced to use their own best judgement in deciding what exact benefits to award. Increasingly, that is, the work is being driven towards level 2.

What happens in practice probably depends much upon the actual calibre of the staff concerned. For those capable of working at level 2, the problem will be to do covertly what it would be more natural to do overtly both in terms of what is called for and what their own abilities can offer. For people who are only capable of level 1 work things will be more difficult. It will not be surprising if feelings of anger and anxiety which derive from an impossible situation – trying desperately to cope with complexities which are in fact beyond one – are not from time to time redirected to clients.

Again there is a clear choice to be faced. Either the whole system of rules must be simplified to the point where benefits due are readily calculable so that the work really can be handled at level 1. Or it must be accepted that discretion is inevitably called for in the assessment of the exact level of individual needs, even though general guidelines may still exist. Again the basic question is the exact sort of service which it is desired to offer. But again too, there are major implications for staffing: whether or not staff of level 1 ability are sufficient, or whether it is essential to recruit (and pay for) people of full level 2 ability.

Personnel and Training Jobs

We have come across various examples of fundamental ambiguities in work level in jobs of so-called 'personnel officers' and 'training officers' with all the consequent problems. The uncertainty here is not just about whether level 1 or level 2 work is required; frequently it may be as between level 2 and level 3 work, or level 3 and level 4 work. Often, where it is agreed that posts of these kinds should be brought into being, those most immediately involved have a fairly ambitious view of what is needed, whilst those in higher authority, with an eye to the salary costs, have another and more limited one.

Perhaps the strongest image of the 'personnel manager' is that of the person (often female) in the factory, office or retail store who interviews applicants for rank-and-file jobs and deals sympathetically with their grievances and personal problems. Such was and is essentially a level 2 job, and its creation marks a significant evolution from the level 1 wages or staffing clerk who merely gives factual answers to people's queries about their pay and conditions of service.

Nowadays, however, specialist personnel posts can arise at a number of other levels. Any factory, office, or similar establishment which employs many hundreds of staff may need a personnel manager working at level 3 (usually with level 2 assistants) whose job is not just to deal with specific problems and disputes as they happen, but to develop better procedures for handling, say, recruitment and selection as a whole, or staff appraisals or regradings, or individual grievances or appeals, or collective disputes or negotiations. A large division, operating company, or public agency employing many thousands of staff, particularly one in which tricky industrial relations issues constantly arise, may need its own 'personnel director' or the equivalent. This will be somebody who is capable of taking a level 4 overview of the field and joining with other colleagues at the same level in the development of corporate policy and strategy. There are no doubt special places where an even higher-level approach to personnel work is called for.

Somewhat the same range of possibilities would appear to arise in training work. A level 1 training job is about giving instruction in set routines. At level 2, by contrast, the work assumes the ability to tailor sessions and teaching to different people or circumstances. A level 3 post may or may not involve its occupant in direct delivery of education and training; the prime task will be to construct, develop, and maintain an effective approach to the training system as a whole. Where a sizeable training centre or college is in existence which provides a comprehensive range of courses there may be scope for a top post at level 4, or even higher.

Research and Development Jobs

The same sort of ambiguity as regards levels often arises in research or development activities as in personnel and training work. Here, as in other fields, uncertainty can sometimes lead to complete failure to tackle necessary work. We came across a striking case of a 'development-officer' post in one social welfare agency which was established in order to pioneer new approaches to the treatment of delinquent adolescents. What was required, it seemed, was a change in the mode of working of the whole department in this particular area – the basis of the level 3 job. What was provided however, was a post which in terms of pay and grade was only likely to bring in a person of level 2 ability. Such a person might well provide leadership on one experimental site. But the formulation and dissemination of general-ised ideas and practices would almost certainly be beyond him or her.

In general, it might be argued that so-called researchers, designers, or development officers at level 2 should always be conceived as assistants to some more-senior person (even more so, any staff at level 1). In the nature of things, the main drive in pioneering or path-breaking activity has to come from those of level 3 capability. Moreover, such level 3 people must have time to be directly immersed in the prime activities concerned, and not forced into some full-time administrative role. As suggested before (in Chapter 5), research and development is not like factory work or routine data processing. The aim should be to arrange things so that the direct output is at level 3 itself, with appropriate *aid* from levels 2 or 1; not a direct output at level 2 or level 1, managed from above.

Secretarial Jobs
When is a secretary a real secretary or when is she (or he) just a shorthand typist, or stenographer, with a fancy title? Sometimes the person who requires a secretarial service is content with someone who can take dictation, type a neat copy, file documents to order, and pass verbatim messages; someone, of course, of good appearance, manner and so on. This is essentially a demand for level 1 work. Often however, the service-receiver wants or needs something more. The 'something more' includes things like using reasonable foresight about future requirements, judging the priorities of current tasks, judging the priorities of requests for appointments, improving poorly-phrased memoranda, filling out cryptic messages, interpreting needs for hotels, entertainment or travel, and so on. This, of course, is essentially level 2 work.

We came across one instance of secretaries in a psychotherapy clinic who were expected to be able to deal with phone calls from existing or would-be patients (all suffering from neurotic disorders of greater or lesser degree) and judge what best initial response to make to their requests. The true level of work demanded here (level 2) was quite unrecognised, and the staff concerned were highly resentful of their inadequate wages and status.

Here, then, is another instance of ambiguous job titles. Senior staff may again often want to exploit the ambiguity so as to keep down salary costs; in other words, they will tend towards a level 1 interpretation of the term 'secretary'. Service-receivers will naturally seek the best service they can, and will tend to a level 2 interpretation.

As in much welfare work, the situation may be further confused by the presence of a large reservoir of available personnel of level 2 ability, including many middle-aged women whose true potential has never been fully recognised, or married women of good capability who are willing to work for low wages. Our own general sense again is of the current existence of considerable numbers of secretaries graded and paid at a level which would suggest level 1 work, but well capable in practice of undertaking work at level 2.

Administrative and Managerial Jobs
The term 'secretary' can of course be applied to work other than at level 1 or level 2 (although it is in respect of these two particular levels that ambiguity is often marked). At one extreme it can apply to a

junior copy-typist. At the other, it can identify the head of the largest State Department (the man who, in times past, had the special ability to translate the King's verbal commands into clear written statements, and hence into coherent action).

Much the same can be said of the terms 'administrator' or 'manager'. Although the discussion of these moves somewhat away from the main focus of this chapter on jobs with a clear selling or service character, a few comments can nevertheless be made at this point.

Both the term 'administrator' and the term 'manager' can, like 'secretary', be applied to the widest range of jobs, from top-level 1 (in special cases) right up to level 7. Some of the enormous variety here is already recognised, in a rough-and-ready way at least, in common usage. Jobs at level 4 and above for example, are often described as 'directorial', or distinguished by the adjective 'general' as in 'general manager', 'general secretary', or (in the army) 'general officer commanding'. At levels 6 or 7 the term 'director general' is sometimes used. And so on. Overall however, the terms 'manager', 'administrator', and 'secretary' are some of the most elastic in the organisational language. The dangers of ambiguous use multiply accordingly.

Conclusions

In this chapter we have looked at a variety of jobs broadly describable as selling or service jobs, in which there are frequent and significant uncertainties as regards required work level. The consequences can be serious if not disastrous. In some cases the organisation may be manifesting major uncertainty about one of the most crucial things: the basic expected work level at the operational front line, the exact level of response to the needs of individual customers or clients (a matter which will have a decisive effect on the ultimate success or failure of the whole enterprise). In other cases there may be a major uncertainty about the exact level of service or impact required from whole internal sections and departments. In all cases there will be a strong likelihood of finding people in posts who are significantly unsuited to what emerges in practice as the predominant demand – either attempting tasks well beyond them, or grossly underemployed.

The work-levels schema can directly help by exposing the main options. In basic secretarial work there will usually be a straight choice between level 1 and level 2. In front-line welfare work there will be a choice between level 1, level 2, or level 2 supported by level 1 aides. In front-line commerical work the usual choice will again be between level 1 and level 2, but with the occasional possibility of level 3. In fields like personnel, training, research and development, the usual choice will be between level 2 and level 3 with the occasional possibility of level 4. Terms like 'manager', 'administrator', or even (in its more general sense) 'secretary' may, unless further qualified, imply almost any possible level of work.

Note
1. The title 'consultant' may often seem a well-fitting one for salesmen and representatives who really to have to operate at level 3 (see comments on this point in Chapter 9). The basic expected work of the fully-fledged 'management consultant' is probably too, at this same level.

9 Professionals in Public Services

The next area in which we are able to provide detailed accounts of the application of the design approach is that of the organisation of professionals employed in public services. Here we draw upon extensive research and development work by ourselves and colleagues in the Brunel Institute of Organisation and Social Studies undertaken over the past fifteen to twenty years in collaboration with doctors, nurses, paramedics, social workers, and various associated administrators and managers.[1] We also draw upon explorations of the individual working situations of many teachers and lecturers (as well as those of further members of the professions just mentioned) who have been following Masters' programmes at Brunel.

The public services in focus are mainly governmental ones, although sometimes provided by voluntary, or even occasionally by private, agencies. The professionals in view can all be thought of as in some way, servants of the public. They tend to express somewhat different concerns to those voiced by groups discussed in the previous chapter who might also claim a professional label – personnel staff or researchers, for example.

In the explorations described, three rather different clusters of problems have in fact regularly emerged. The first centre around *professional autonomy*. On the one hand, the professionals concerned frequently feel their legitimate freedom to be under attack; under attack from higher managers or (in some cases) members of other professions. Doctors for example, express alarm when administrators start to question their rate of throughput of patients, or expenditure on drugs. Trained social workers feel aggrieved at their cases being scrutinised by elected politicians, or their financial allocations to clients having to be approved by senior staff. Nurses feel resentful when doctors intrude into issues of ward management.

On this same subject of autonomy, however, others concerned – administrators, governors, fellow workers, even (sometimes) recipients of service – often express the view that these professionals are allowed far too much freedom. Why (they ask) should professionals not be subject to public accountability and normal managerial controls like the rest? Why should they be given so much licence to pursue their own particular ideas, to promote their own idiosyncratic values?

The second general problem area for professionals in public services concerns *career and progression.* Only too often, it seems, individual practitioners find themselves faced with a cruel dilemma: to stay in practice and relinquish any prospects of more money and status, or to opt for promotion, but in doing so to move out of practice into administration, and thus in effect to cease being a professional. Social workers who want to progress sometimes find themselves forced to give up their personal caseload. Teachers in the same situation have to leave the classroom. Nurses have to leave the ward.

The third main set of problems encountered in our work with public-service professionals are not peculiar to the latter, but are nevertheless burdensome. They are the classic ones which spring from *weak or badly conceived management systems;* from the confusion of grading stuctures with management structures, the failure to separate main managerial roles from staff and supervisory ones, and the failure to establish the right number of management levels.

In this chapter we start by describing how work-level and related ideas bear upon the particular problems of doctors, nurses, para-medics, social workers, and teachers, looking at each group in turn. Then we develop a general model of the main steps in professional work, discussing how autonomy, career progression and managerial control may most appropriately be handled at each.

The Organisation of Doctors
From our work with doctors, the main problems centre without doubt around the vexed question of *autonomy.*[2] (We focus here primarily upon hospital and specialist doctors in the British National Health Service. General medical practitioners in the NHS are not employees in the legal sense but contractors, and their organisation is closer to private practice.) Doctors exercise extensive power and freedom, and, seen from the patients' point of view, this is reassuring. But doctors are also directly or indirectly, the initiators of virtually all workload, all development, and all expenditure. If each is allowed to pursue his or her own path unguided and untramelled (which often appears to be close to the situation in reality) then the result from a management viewpoint can be chaos.

Looking at work levels helps to locate the problems more exactly. For a start, it emphasises the crucial difference between the situation of consultants and junior doctors. The latter, the house officers, senior house officers, registrars and senior registrars (interns as they would be called in other countries), work at various points in level 2. Two stages of training are involved within these grades, the first leading to registration as a basic medical practitioner, and the second to a higher specialist qualification. Although all such junior doctors have, in some degree, freedom to make their own assessments and prescribe their own treatments in individual cases, all clearly work under the direction of the consultant who sets general rules and policies. At this point there is no great issue of autonomy or control: the consultant is in effect the main line-manager and, like other managers, delegates responsibility and authority as judged best: more to so-called registrars and less to so-called house officers. The former often act in a *supervisory* role (as earlier defined) to the latter.

Our work has clearly shown that the expectation in the consultant post itself is level 3: not just to treat individual patients one by one, but to provide and develop a systematic service in the speciality concerned – surgery, obstetrics, psychiatry or whatever. (Where individual consultants possess or develop personal abilities for work beyond level 3, as is not infrequently the case, these often become manifested in medical administration, or extensive research or teaching activities.)

It is at level 3, in fact, where the real problem of autonomy in medicine arises. Of course, doctors or any other practitioners at level 3 should be expected to be expert in their own subjects, and should expect in turn to have a large measure of freedom not only to deal with their own cases but to devise and develop their own techniques. But why, it might very well be asked, should there not exist level 4 managers of consultants, with ultimate rights, even if rarely used, to zoom into clinical work, make appraisals of quality or output, prescribe technical methods of procedures, and set guiding priorities and policies? Such managers (the argument proceeds) could not be expected to be more expert in every field than their subordinates; but then, managers at this level rarely are.

The case for senior doctors being left free from reviews by some managerial superior in respect of their *clinical* work is a special one. It is based on the argument that any such reviews, and consequent pre-scriptions, could not be undertaken without destroying the necessary trust and confidence between doctor and patient – that they would strike at the very root of the doctor–patient relationship. This argument cannot be further discussed or evaluated here.[3] But even if it holds up, what it does not imply should be clearly noted as well as what it does.

Clinical autonomy, in the sense just described, does not imply that any attempt whatsoever to control or influence the work of senior doctors is illegitimate. There may not be scope for straightforward main line-managers. But, as suggested earlier (Chapter 5), somebody in a large health-service organisation needs to be undertaking level 4 (and higher-level) thinking in respect of medical work, whether it is done by an individual or a group, by lay people or the medically qualified. Somebody should be deciding when to give doctors more resources and when to give them less (not in itself an interference in clinical autonomy). Somebody (arguably) should be monitoring the adherence of doctors to their employment contracts, to acceptable standards of clinical practice, and to reasonable standards of personal behaviour and civility. Somebody (arguably) should be exercising normal co-ordinative authority (as earlier defined) in the implement-ation of any such policies or projects as are generally agreed. Somebody (arguably) should be responsible for persuading doctors to engage in their own collective reviews of methods and results. Discussion of detailed mechanisms here is beyond the present text, but the basic needs seem clear enough.

A work-levels approach, then, does not by itself solve the question of medical autonomy, but it at least pinpoints where the real issue arises, namely in the level 3 (medical consultant) post. And it indicates some of the necessary work in medical management which still has to be done at higher levels even if the same level 3 doctors are granted freedom in exactly how they respond to the needs of individual patients.

A work-levels approach also throws some new light on *career paths* in medicine. Specialist medicine provides in fact one of the best examples of a profession where progression to level 3 whilst still in professional practice is both possible and expected. But there are still some problems. There is the debate about the necessity, or otherwise, for permanent sub-consultant grades. The issue can be seen to be that of whether or not to provide career posts (as opposed to training posts) at level 2 in hospital and specialist work for those who do not wish, or do not have the ability, to take on full level 3 responsibilities. And there is the question (touched on earlier) of how exactly to provide adequate scope and rewards for those doctors with a general ability for level 4 work or beyond, whether their interests are still primarily clinical or more broadly administrative.

The Organisation of Nurses
From our work with nurses it would appear that the main organ-isational problems are usually to do with *weak management structures*, although concerns about career paths and autonomy are

far from absent.[4] A fundamental issue is the basic work level expected of any qualified nurse. Is the training which leads to statutory registration (as opposed to the training for enrolment status, or as a nursing aide) designed to produce fully-fledged professionals capable of making their own responses to complex situations, that is, to operate at level 2? Or is merely intended to produce a body of top-level 1 technicians capable of carrying out a wide range of prescribed nursing procedures (some of whom may subsequently develop into level 2)? The answer carries major implications for recruitment, and for the form of the training or educational process itself. But it also deeply affects management arrangements, particularly at ward level; and relations with medical staff.

As regards the latter, nurses often express resentment at what they see as the over-authoritative position adopted by doctors, particularly the more senior ones. But, as just suggested, the position is greatly affected by whether the qualified nurse is seen by senior doctors as a subordinate technician at level 1, or as a fellow, albeit junior, professional at level 2. In the first case, although doctors will not usually aspire to a main line-management relation to nurses, with its implicit responsibility for such things as recruitment, training, support, and career development, they will nevertheless carry clear prescribing authority (as defined in Chapter 2) and tend, moreover, to apply it to a wide range of concerns. In the second case, although doctors may still lay down definite prescriptions on treatment, in other respects the relationship will start to feel far closer to a collateral one (as earlier defined), in which the two parties work together in the interests of the patient, each having a different and largely complementary task, but neither having authority over the other.

As regards ward organisation, there are regular complaints that the role of the ward sister is not what is used to be, and equally regular proposals that its managerial character should be re-emphasised and strengthened. There is a good case here perhaps. But in defining just what the managerial role of the ward sister means and exactly how far it extends, the expected work level of the qualified nurse is again of considerable significance. If it is only level 1, there is scope for a straightforward main line-management role at level 2 for the ward sister, with full managerial authority in respect of all other nursing staff who work on the ward, day or night (see Figure 9.1(a)). If the basic qualified nursing post is itself at level 2, however, then the situation inevitably becomes more complex (see Figure 9.1(b)). The ward sister may act with *supervisory* authority in relation to any qualified nurses simultaneously on duty, or *monitoring and coordinating* authority to qualified nurses on duty at other times, but

Figure 9.1 Alternative models of ward organisation

(a) Qualified nurses work basically at level 1

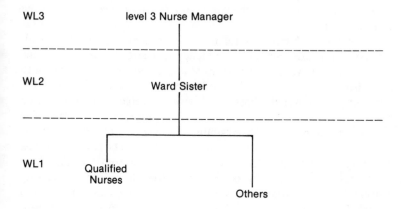

(b) Qualified nurses work basically at level 2

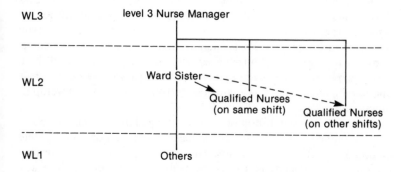

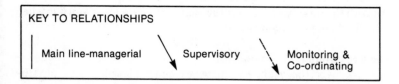

elements of the management of all qualified nurses on the ward – the crucial judgements on their overall capabilities, their needs for further training or extended responsibilities, or their claims to upgrading or promotion – will all have to be undertaken by some level 3 nurse manager who operates beyond the ward. However, the ward sister can still carry an unqualified main line-management role in relation to nursing aides or others on the ward who undertake prescribed-output work at level 1.

Nursing in the NHS from the time of the Salmon Report[5] onwards provides many examples of the tendency, discussed in earlier chapters, to confuse *management structures* with *grading structures* and both (moreover) with *job titles*. The following example may illustrate the last point. Whatever the basic work level expected of other qualified nurses, that expected of the ward sister appears (from extensive discussion) to be level 2. Arguably, in wards where complex or technically advanced work is carried out it ought to be able to attract a grade right at the top of this level. But the current top-level 2 grade in the NHS is decribed as a 'nursing officer'. And (by definition) nursing officers do not run individual wards. So ward sisters, even those who clearly deserve it, cannot be paid at a rate commensurate with top-level 2 work.

The confusion of grading structures and management structures is often particularly evident above ward level. Perhaps the worst result (apart from the depression of ward sister posts just mentioned) is the common failure to develop solid main line-management posts at level 3 with substantial and sensibly bounded areas of responsibility, and to separate these from any necessary staff-officer posts (of the type discussed in Chapter 5). Posts such as 'nursing officer', 'senior nurse' and 'assistant director of nursing services' proliferate, but few of these (in our experience) are currently defined in such a way as to allow clear and unequivocal main line-management roles at level 3 to develop in practice.

Given a proper separation of grades, titles and management levels in nursing (added to clarity about the basic expected work level of the qualified nurse), it becomes possible to develop clearer ward organisation, better prospects for those who wish to remain in ward management and stronger, simpler management structures at levels above. The realisation of any or all of these things cannot help but improve the quality of the eventual service to patients – which is what it is all, of course, finally about.

The Organisation of Paramedics

In work over the years by ourselves and colleagues with physiotherapists, occupational therapists, clinical psychologists, radiographers and members of other paramedical groups, issues of *autonomy*, *management* and *career paths* have all regularly surfaced.[6] Should individual practitioners be allowed to get on with treatments as they think best, once cases have been referred to them? What authority should doctors, or more senior staff in their own disciplines, have over them, and what management structure is appropriate? How far should it be possible to travel in career terms, whilst still remaining in direct practice?

As for nurses, the crucial issue is the basic level of work expected of the fully-trained practitioner. Answers would appear to vary significantly from group to group, and sometimes also to have shifted within any particular group as the years have gone by. In radiography, for example, the basic expectation now, as in the past, appears to be no more than for skilled level 1 work. In physiotherapy, by contrast, the expectation now seems firmly set in level 2. As regards clinical psychology, a publication by leading members of the profession in Britain couched in explicit work-level terms, argues that the target career grade should be seen as level 3.[7] Whatever the answer reached in any particular case, it has again profound implications for selection and training, for autonomy, and for professional organisation and career paths.

Where the basic expected work is level 1, paramedical staff are in effect being recruited, trained and employed as specialist medical auxiliaries. As such, they may expect to work under direct medical prescription. If doctors themselves do not actually manage them there is no bar to one of their own number of suitable ability acting in a straightforward level 2 management role. Opportunities for professional practice (so-called) will be restrained within level 1.

Where the basic expected work is level 2, quite a different sort of trainee will have to be looked for. Qualified paramedical staff will expect scope within referred cases, to make judgements of their own about appropriate treatment. There will be room to employ aides or assistants at level 1 to carry out specific bits of treatment or investigation that can be readily prespecified. (Such auxiliary staff already exist, for example, in physiotherapy and occupational therapy.) Teams may develop with top-level 2 leaders who have to carry a complex of different roles and realtionships to other members. Principal or superintendent posts at level 3 may be created where there are large numbers of basic practitioners to be looked after. The former may themselves continue part-time in direct practice, and will, appropriately, carry rights to set general policies, on clinical practice, as well as to control workload.

Where the basic expected work is level 3 (a situation which is perhaps for the moment largely hypothetical) then appropriate organisation might well begin to resemble that described earlier for specialist medical practice. The career structure would culminate in full-scale consultant-practitioner posts. All level 2 practitioners would presumably be under the direct control of such level 3 consultants. There would appear no scope for posts at either level 2 or level 3 with the title 'principal' or 'superintendent'.

As regards any given group of paramedical staff, then, recruitment and training, career structures, relations with doctors, and management structures, will all crucially depend on the central question of the basic expected work level. (How this last is to be decided, however, may not by any means be a simple matter: the professions concerned will have one view, but in the end, it may be argued, it is up to employing authorities to decide what they want, agree to, or are willing to pay for.) Given a statement of basic expected work level, specific formulations may be developed in relation to each of the topics just mentioned. But no one model is likely to serve for all the groups which are gathered under the broad paramedical rubric. This is the general message here.

The Organisation of Social Workers

In our work over the years with social workers in local authority departments in Great Britain, problems of both *autonomy* and *management* have again regularly emerged[8] (opportunities for extended *career paths* in professional practice have tended to improve in recent years). There can be little doubt that the basic expected work level in the great majority of professional social work posts is level 2, and there is now often a range of different grades available within this broad level. Occasional practitioner posts graded in such a way as to suggest an expectation of level 3 work are to be found in specialist areas like child guidance or community work. Much of the front-line activity in current British social welfare agencies is carried out, however (as discussed in the previous chapter), not by professional social workers, but by care attendants, home helps and the like, many of whose jobs are pitched at level 1.

The answer to the question of how much freedom should be allowed to social workers, or alternatively, how much control and supervision should be exercised over them, is crucially related to just what level of so-called social worker is in mind. For those definitely operating in level 1, clear prescription of detailed results required should be available in all cases. To offer less is to leave any worker whose personal ability is limited to this level in a highly unsatisfactory and anxiety-provoking situation. For those in the process of transition to level 2, students, trainees and newly-qualified workers, some freedom – gradually increasing – to make their own assessments is necessary and appropriate, but frequent and positive supervision is imperative. For main-grade and senior workers, professional supervision should no longer be necessary, but formal review of crucial case decisions, the opportunity for voluntary consultation with more experienced workers, and the presence of appraisal, support and scene-setting by a level 3 manager will all be desirable. For practitioners operating at level 3, any professional supervision would seem wholly inappropriate, and even formal review perhaps uncalled for as well. However, a continuing, if intermittent, link is still necessary with some managers at level 4.

Moving to management, there are commonly problems at several levels. The role of team leaders is particularly tricky. For a start there is uncertainty about the expected work level of the job. The traditional role probably has no more than a top-level 2 expectation of work. However, recent trends in practice towards greater decentralisation, geographical 'patch' operation, and more integrated groupings of domiciliary, day, and residential services, have all combined to push the work expected to the team leader up into level 3. In either event the fact that social workers may, as just described, be operating at so many different practice levels, places any team leader in a complex situation.

If the assumption is made (see Figure 9.2) that the team leader should operate at level 2 a main line-managerial relation to any aides or other staff at level 1 is quite appropriate. Newly-qualified social workers may need professional supervision. All team members will need co-ordination as regards specific work-programmes, and monitoring as regards their adherence to established policies and practices. But all professional social workers (or at any rate, all reasonably well-established ones) are likely to be looking beyond a level 2 team leader in regard to any more fundamental management of their current jobs and prospects (there is an obvious parallel here with the nursing situation just described). If the assumption is made that the team leader post is pitched at level 3, the whole scene changes again. (Given this uncertainty and complexity, it is no surprise that many team leaders are felt to be, or feel themselves to be, insecure in their jobs.)

As regards more-senior management posts in social work, there appear to be several characteristic weaknesses. Where the job of a so-called area officer involves looking after a few teams of field social workers, and that alone, it seems to sit solidly at level 3. But where

Figure 9.2 A possible model of social work team organisation

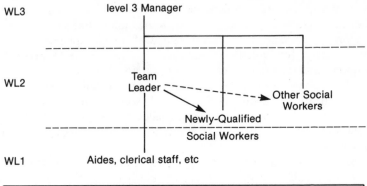

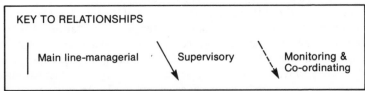

greater responsibilities are delegated to team leaders, forcing them up towards level 3, and where (as is often the case) the area officer is expected to look after ever-extended combinations of fieldworkers, residential workers, and day-centre and domiciliary workers, the area officer's own job becomes increasingly difficult to encompass at level 3 and begins to push (other things allowing) into level 4.

Where residential and day care are organised in a separate division or separate divisions, our explorations have frequently revealed an almost complete absence of effective level 3 management (see Figure 9.3). Heads of divisions, in larger agencies at least, are usually heavily involved in level 4 work; heads of individual establishments (homes or day centres) are mostly working at level 2. So-called 'home advisers' or 'day-care advisers' shown between the two on official charts, are often given little real authority or responsibility, and turn out only too frequently to be personally capable of no more than level 2 work.

The Organisation of Teachers

In our various discussions with schoolteachers, the organisational problems most commonly cited are those of *unclear or ineffective management structures*, particularly as regards the position of heads of departments, heads of year, and heads of house, or the like

Figure 9.3 Typical missing management level in residential/day-care divisions in large welfare agencies

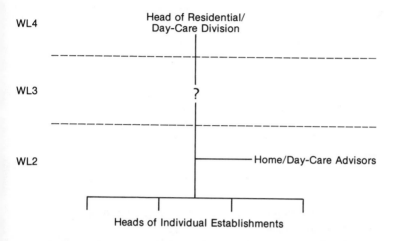

(although there are no doubt parallel issues of autonomy and career progression).

By way of a start, it seems fair to assume that all qualified teachers today, even those in primary or nursery schools, are expected to operate at least at level 2. (Those who are expected only to teach or train at level 1 are perhaps best described as 'instructors' or 'teaching aides'.) In junior schools, the post of head teacher seems to be pitched at level 3, and it appears easy for a straightforward main line-managerial relationship to develop between the head and all other teaching staff, with the former in a clear position to give instructions on curriculum and methods.

However, in secondary schools, which are usually much larger, the situation is different. Here, the expectation on the head seems not just that of running a given teaching facility systematically (level 3) but of developing a comprehensive range of educational programmes of some given kind (level 4). Given basic teaching posts at level 2, there is space for some intermediate management level (see Figure 9.4). In practice, certain head-of-department, head-of-year, or head-of-house posts do appear to be pitched at level 3, but others only at level 2. The latter could not conceivably provide the necessary intermediate structure. But even for those in level 3 posts it is usually far from evident which, if any, are expected to play main line-managerial roles in relation to level 2 teachers, and which are merely expected to

Figure 9.4 Typical unclear middle-management structures in large secondary schools

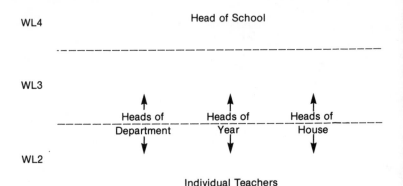

undertake some monitoring or co-ordinating role in respect of their particular fields of concern.

Discussion with various staff from colleges of further education suggest not dissimilar problems (higher education, in universities and polytechnics, is probably quite different, however[9]). Basic lecturer roles appear to be pitched at level 2. Head of department roles appear to be pitched in some cases at level 3 and in others at level 4. In either event there are often hierarchies of posts of intermediate grade whose authority and responsibility are more or less problematic – group heads, subject heads, programme head, and so on.

The main thing to be emphasised here is again the crucial difference between grades and management levels. Where heads of department are at level 4 there is room for just one intermediate main management level, and where at Level 3, room for none. Many of the roles just described will thus be more realistically seen in many cases as co-ordinating ones rather than main line-managerial.

A General Model of Professional Organisation

Drawing on the various explorations of professional organisation just described, we have developed a general model of the main steps in professional work, as shown in Figure 9.5. Each step carries its own distinct implications for autonomy and control. Overall, a clear pattern of alternative career paths becomes evident.

For any job fixed wholly within level 1 it is something of a misnomer to describe the work as 'professional'. All professionals worth their salt must be able and willing to make their own independ-

Figure 9.5 Main steps in professional work

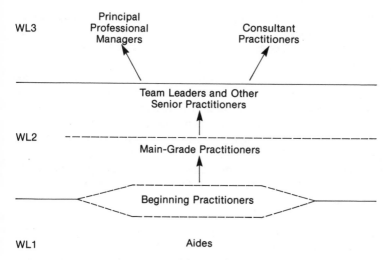

ent appraisals of new and compex situations; to penetrate beyond surface demands to real needs.[10] But this is precisely what is not required at level 1, the level where production follows automatically upon given stimuli or demands. Staff here, however service-orientated their attitudes, technical their backgrounds, or skilled their abilities, are better described as *aides, technicians* or *craftsmen*, than professionals.

Thus level 2 is the first level of real professional activity. But there appear to be three natural subdivisions (a fact which has obvious implications for possible grading structures). In the first subdivision are what may be called the *beginning practitioners* (the junior house doctor, the student nurse, the newly qualified social worker and so on), some studying still for their formal qualifications, some in the first year or two after gaining them. The situation of such people is finely balanced. (They may be shown pictorially as in the transition zone between level 1 and level 2.) On the one hand it is essential to let them experience for themselves the demanding task of sizing up complex situations and shaping actions accordingly. In other words, they must be allowed to try out for themselves some 'situational response' work – regularly and increasingly, as their skill and confidence develops. On the other hand they will often need firm guidance and presciption in difficult cases. Support must be readily available on demand. And there must be regular appraisal in retrospect of work already done. At this stage, there is as ready a danger of allowing too much autonomy as too little. Professional staff at this first level need regular professional supervision.

If things go as they ought, however, a time comes, perhaps after a year or two of experience under such regular supervision, when the professional person concerned is now ready to stand on his or her own feet. In many professions this point is marked by public registration, or by a move into a new class of membership in the professional association (this is sometimes a different, and later, point than the one at which necessary academic qualifications are first achieved). As far as the employing organisation is concerned, this is often an appropriate point to arrange an upgrading to what may be generally, or even specifically, described as *main-grade practitioner* (although in branches of professional work like specialist medicine, where the target is level 3 work, this particular post might be thought of as 'basic grade' rather than 'main grade' perhaps). The person concerned is now judged to be a fully-fledged professional, able to carry out professional work independently (indeed, to be competent to set up in private practice should he or she wish). There may still be a need for occasional advice or consultation, but no longer a need for regular supervision, at least as regards professional technique. Something will be wrong if the practitioners concerned are not left to get on with their own clients, patients, pupils, cases, or whatever. However, this does not imply that there should be no review or monitoring at all of their activities. Nor does it imply that it is inappropriate for managers at level 3 to be setting general systems or policies – quite the contrary.

In many organisations there is evidently some need to allow for yet another possible change in status. After further years of experience, involving perhaps the gaining of special knowledge and skill in particular fields, and futher or more specialised qualifications, the practitioner is seen as capable of undertaking some qualitatively different and more-complex class of work, although still broadly within level 2. The change may be marked by a further upgrading. Conceptually, such people may now be thought of as *senior practitioners*. Often it will be just these who provide regular supervision for beginning practitioners. Sometimes they may be given the job of acting as working leaders of small professional groups (like team leaders in social work or ward sisters in nursing, for example). Sometimes they may work mainly on their own. There is a choice.

In either case however, there will be many professionals whose personal development does not stop or peak in level 2. For those willing and able to operate at level 3 one possibility which is frequently open is that of taking over a full-scale management job with responsibility for a much wider group of level 2 practitioners and level 1 aides and clerical staff; say, all those in a particular department, office, school or speciality. Posts at this higher level often carry the title 'principal' or 'head'. They may be described generically as those of *principal professional managers.*

Being at level 3, the prime responsibility in posts of this latter kind is to maintain and develop the system as a whole, bearing in mind such things as new trends in professional practice, changing patterns of workload, and both the possibilities and constraints presented by the particular people and resources currently available. Those in such posts may often need to 'zoom' into cases of special difficulty or uncertainty faced by their level 2 subordinates, but they may often find it difficult to carry on with any direct professional practice of their own. Essentially, these jobs are to manage a stream of level 2 outputs produced by others.

The other possibility, one often veiled by the wrong (but common) assumption that any move to a higher grade must necessarily represent a move into management, is that of creating practitioner posts which are themselves pitched at level 3 (like the medical consultant). Any practitioners at this advanced level would be expected not only to be handling individual cases or tasks in an expert way, but to be well abreast of new thinking, and constantly developing their own systems and practice as they go on. Conversely, people capable of such work are likely to be just those who make the main contribution to the advancement of knowledge in the profession concerned. Reflections on the general pattern of their own experience and the systematic basis of their own practice, will often provide material for talks, teaching and the production of papers and articles. Such people will be natural participants in general reviews of current practice, or the planning of new developments, as well as providers to other, more junior, professionals of advice on out-of-the-ordinary problems. People of this latter type may be thought of in general as *consultant practitioners.* Although it is quite possible for them to operate completely on their own, they may sometimes be supported by one or two assistants in level 2. However, their jobs are not mainly about managing a stream of level 2 outputs produced by others, but of producing themselves, or with a little aid, a direct level 3 output.

The management of consultant practitioners will itself be appropriately pitched at level 4. It will be difficult for higher-level managers, even those of the same professional background, to issue effective instructions either about the best action in any individual case or about the best procedures or methods to use in general. Nevertheless, higher management will always have the rights to set or reset general aims and duties, to allocate or reallocate resources, and to monitor outcomes. And usually, higher management will have the right to set binding policies as well – give more attention to this, play down that – although this may not hold where such a right is inconsistent for example with clinical autonomy (as in medicine) or freedom of thought (as in higher academic teaching or academic research).

Where professional posts are themselves pitched at level 4 in large employing organisations, the work would appear almost invariably to be completely administrative or managerial in character. Frequent and extended meetings are usually called for with other top officers to consider corporate plans, problems, and financing. Usually, too, there are large divisions of subordinate staff to be managed. The scope for direct professional work is usually insignificant. Anybody whose personal ability and experience has qualified them to work at this level (or higher ones still) and who is determined to remain doing direct professional work is thus probably obliged to turn from regular employment to private practice of some kind: to go into a partnership perhaps, or to go freelance, or to act as an independent consultant.[11]

Conclusion

In this chapter we have seen how the basic design approach applies to the organisation of professionals in public services. A general model has been developed which indicates the sort of autonomy and management which is appropriate at various steps in professional work and how this changes from one step to the next. It also helps to reveal the full variety of potential career paths. On the first score it underlines the impossibility of simple or blanket answers to the question of how much autonomy professionals should be allowed. On the second, it emphasises that higher grades do not necessarily have to incur major managerial responsibilities; and that posts in which the main emphasis is on direct professional practice should often be a possibility at quite advanced grades – usually up to the top of level 2, and sometimes beyond into level 3.

We would assume that the model has relevance not only to the particular professional groups discussed here, but to other professionals regularly to be found in employment in both the public and the private sectors: for example, engineers, designers, architects and accountants. It may also have some relevance to the police service.[12] In all these cases we would suppose that real professional practice does not start until level 2, and that any level 1 jobs are sub-professional ones. In each we would suppose that the same issue arises of marking in some way the distinction between trainees, main-grade practitioners and senior practitioners – all in level 2. And in each we would suppose that there is a very real issue of the possible practitioner posts (as opposed to management posts) in level 3. Once again, it all depends on what sort of front-line impact it is required to make on the external° world, on what level of direct service is looked for in relation to individual clients or patients.

Notes

1. The three main published accounts of this work are: E. Jaques, ed., *Health Services*, 1978; D. Billis, G. Bromley, A. Hey and R. Rowbottom, *Organising Social Services Departments*, London, Heinemann, 1980, and D. Billis, *Welfare Bureaucracies*, London, Heinemann, 1984. For earlier work, see R.W. Rowbottom *et al.*, *Hospital Organisation*, London, Heinemann, 1973; and R.W. Rowbottom, A.M. Hey and D. Billis, *Social Services Departments: Developing Patterns of Work and Organisation*, London, Heinemann, 1974. See also the various other publications referred to in notes 2, 6 and 8 below. An extensive literature exists on the subject of professionals in public-service bureaucracies, including notable work by Amitai Etzioni, Peter Blau and W.R. Scott. But its focus is almost exclusively on the provision of general sociological insight rather than direct practical guidance.
2. See Rowbottom *et al.*, *Hospital Organisation*, Chapter 5; Jaques, *Health Services*, Chapters 1, 3, 4 and 5; and W. Kinston, 'Resource Consumption and Future Organisation of Medical Work in the National Health Service', *Social Science and Medicine*, vol 16, 1982, pp. 1619–26.
3. For further discussion see Rowbottom *et al.*, *Hospital Organisation*; Jaques, *Health Services*; and Kinston, 'Resource Consumption'.
4. See Rowbottom *et al.*, *Hospital Organisation*, Chapter 7.
5. Ministry of Health, *Report of the Committee on Senior Nurse Staff Structure* (Salmon Report), London, HMSO, 1966.
6. See Rowbottom *et al.*, *Hospital Organisation*, Chapter 6; Jaques, *Health Services*, Chapters 5, 9 and 10; the series of five articles on the organisation of physiotherapy work by W. Kinston, J. Øvretveit and others in *Physiotherapy*, vols 67–68, 1981–2; *and* J. Øvretveit, 'Organising Psychology in the NHS', A Health Services Centre Working Paper, Brunel Institute of Organisation and Social Studies, 1984.
7. D. Thomas, B. Kat and F. McPherson, 'Clinical Psychology, An Independent Profession', *Health and Social Services Journal*, 23 May 1980.
8. See Rowbottom *et al.*, *Social Services Departments*, Billis *et al.*, *Organising Social Services Departments*, and Billis, *Welfare Bureaucracies*; also A. Hey, 'Social Work – Practice, Careers and Organisation in Area Teams', A Social Services Unit Working Paper, Brunel Institute of Organisation and Social Studies, 1978.
9. From our own direct experience in universities, the proposition would be that the expected work in the basic lecturer post is in fact level 3, in providing and developing a systematic approach to particular topics. Senior lecturers and professors are probably expected to work at least at level 4, in providing and organising comprehensive teaching or research programmes across complete subject areas. If so, the jump from lecturer to senior lecturer is highly significant, and there is no reason to suppose that everybody recruited to the profession can be expected to make it. It follows that any proposal (as currently arises) for a grading system which ignores or blurs the jump is probably badly misjudged.
10. Indeed work levels throw a new element into the vexed question of what *defines* a profession or professional. Many criteria have been suggested by commentators on the subject: a need for prolonged basic training; rigorous tests of knowledge and competence before qualification; a system of public regulation or accreditation; the existence of a professional association; the existence of some explicit code of

behaviour with a real possibility of disbarment; a prime orientation to service rather than profit; the possession of some special body of knowledge and skill. (Others, more cynically, have suggested that professions are simply the groups that have got on top and managed to keep on top, by various exercises of power and control.) What the work-levels approach adds is the idea that true professionals must be expected to make their own independent assessment of, and responses to, the needs of complex situations facing them (a level 2 or higher response), as opposed simply to carrying out set tasks, with whatever degree of skill and expertise (a level 1 response).

11. It is notable that journalists, TV producers and the like move increasingly into freelance work as they achieve personal prominence in their various fields. It is also notable that opportunity is always made available for senior academics to develop their careers and supplement their earnings through private work of various kinds. Academia may however be one place where direct professional practice at level 4 is still possible – see note 9 above.

12. From personal observations, and occasional discussion with police officers, we are struck by two things. The first thing is the ambiguity in the basic job as it currently stands: is it a prescribed-output one (as in routine traffic control, or the physical restraint of members of unruly crowds) or a situational-response one (as in 'community policing')? The second thing is the classic confusion of grades – sergeant, inspector, chief inspector and so on – with management structures, with all its attendant ill-feeling and malfunction.

10 Top Structures in Industry and Commerce

In this chapter various applications of the design approach to top structures in industry and commerce are described. 'Top structures' is taken here to mean those at work level 4 and upward (although, of course, those at the head of level 3 – or even level 2 – enterprises are entitled in a sense to describe themselves as in 'top' posts). In developing this theme we draw upon work already mentioned in four large industrial concerns (in the fields of engineering, household appliances, chemical and metal processing) and in two insurance companies. We also draw upon detailed discussions within our Brunel workshops with senior representatives of some twenty or so other industrial firms and public utilities, two large retail organisations, three banks, another insurance company and a building society. In all these explorations, issues of top-management structure have regularly come to the fore.

The main thing to emerge is without doubt the strong impression of cluttered hierarchies – *far too many levels of management in the higher reaches just as in the lower ones.* General managers jostle for places with operations directors, managing directors, presidents and chairmen. Local sales staff find above them extended hierarchies of area sales managers, regional sales managers, general sales managers, and sales or marketing directors. Production superintendents find that they have to report to works managers, who have to report to general works managers, who have to report to production managers, who have in turn to report to directors of manufacturing. At very top levels, chief executives of operating companies themselves stagger under elaborate superstructures of holding companies, divisional boards, regional boards, and continental boards. Throughout all, various deputies, assistants and coordinators struggle to establish their own particular rungs on the ladder as well.

In this chapter we shall concentrate on three particular areas where proliferation of levels and confusion of responsibilities seem to be regular and marked (without suggesting that these are the only or main ones). The first is the large or super-large manufacturing facility on one extended site which, whether or not it carries the status of a registered company in its own right, is really part of some larger operating division. The second is the structure of regional and sub-regional management frequently to be found in insurance, banking and similar enterprises as a bridge between headquarters and a large scatter of local offices or branches. The third (to be looked at more briefly) is the typical many-layered geographical organisation that arises at the top of large multinational corporations.

Large Manufacturing Sites

We have already discussed in Chapter 7 a range of possible models of factory organisation culminating respectively at work levels, 2, 3 and 4. What happens when the site is so large and the manufacturing operation so complex that it looks as though the top executive post needs to be at level 5?

Plant A was a large complex with an annual turnover of £500 million which employed over two thousand people in some forty separate production units. It belonged to a major corporation with world-wide operations. Discussions revealed the usual problems of cluttered hierarchies. As a result of project work on site it was eventually agreed that four main management-levels could be distinguished: foremen or section leaders (level 2); production managers in charge of separate units, or section engineers (level 3); heads of major departments (level 4), and the works manager in overall control (level 5). Heads of department were of two kinds: heads of groups of production units, and heads of various groups of supporting services like process technology, maintenance and construction, personnel, and accounting.

There seemed little doubt that the various heads of department were indeed expected to operate at level 4. We found that their job descriptions were replete with phrases like 'assessing future assets requirements in order to meet business requirements', 'ensuring the correct balance and spread of professional skills to provide continuing personnel resources in the future', '[developing] comprehensive plans and budgets to meet current and future business needs'. And, given a solid layer of such level 4 posts, it would certainly appear that a works manager post at level 5 would be necessary.

But what would constitute the actual content of level 5 work in such a post? As the title suggests, it did not span functions other than manufacturing ones. All marketing, commercial and product-development functions were in a quite separate part of the organisation. Moreover, it was stressed in the documents which introduced the redefined organisation that it was up to the various heads of department, not the works manager, to undertake the bulk of disussions with senior commercial and product-development colleagues about general strategies for future business operations. Here then was a major unresolved problem.

Plant B was part of another multinational corporation employing some thousand or so staff using a highly-automated technology. It was formally established as a company in its own right. Once again, however, its own top management was concerned purely with manufacturing and manufacturing methods, and had little or no direct responsibility for marketing or basic product development. In discussion, much reference was made to problems in the relationships with the next tier of the organisation, the regional headquarters, situated some hundreds of miles away. Headquarters staff were felt to be constantly eating into the job of running the plant. It was impossible for the works director in charge to develop any sort of strategic plan of his own. After a discussion of work levels, one of the senior staff commented 'we pretended that plants like these are companies, but they have no level 5 work to do'. An interesting point was also made that all the essential data for level 5 planning were available only at regional headquarters.

The general question to emerge from the two examples just cited may be put as follows: it is really possible to set up effective posts at level 5 in a particular function like manufacturing; and if so, what exactly does the work consist of?

Now, it is certainly possible in organisations of appropriate size to establish manufacturing posts at level 4. The essential job at this level is to develop and maintain a comprehensive production facility for the specific range of products currently on offer or likely to be called for within a coming time period of, say, up to four or five years. In deciding what future products to make provision for, strong linkage is demanded with parallel staff in research, development and marketing. The concern in a level 4 production job is comprehensive and future-looking, but it is still firmly based in consideration of specific ranges of products of known or definable types. But how does one undertake (as would be implicit at level 5) a development of some general *field* of production, without too much thought about specific product types?

In any level 5 job in industry the natural tendency is to consider not just possible manufacturing developments on their own in relation to any given field (footwear, say, or audio-visual equipment, or fertilisers or mining machinery); or, for that matter, possible developments on their own in product design or marketing. It is to consider all three of these basic and complementary activities together and as a whole: manufacturing, marketing, and product development. And, it is equally natural therefore, at level 5, to bring all three strands into the hands of one chief executive.

Where a chief executive has responsibility for the whole business, not just for manufacturing separately, or marketing, or product development, then he or she can reasonably be held responsible for profit. And, it becomes easy and logical to establish an operating company with its own profit-and-loss account and balance sheet. After all, business is not just a question of producing, or selling, or conceiving new products. It is a matter of doing all three together and in the right balance: a question of earning profits by making the most attractive products by the most efficient methods and offering them to the right people at the right price and in the right way.

If in any given post there is no such possibility of managing some combination of manufacturing, marketing and product development, or even of the first two alone, any suggestion of a separate business or profit centre must be strongly questioned. The use of 'transfer costs' to allow the calculation of the notional profits generated by a particular function is usually in our experience regarded with extreme suspicion by those at the receiving end – rightly so, in view of the arbitrary accounting assumptions often having to be made. In large organisations like the ones under discussion, the conception of separate businesses is usually unrealistic at level 3 or below simply because there is rarely anybody at such levels whose job does or could span a sufficient range of functions. At level 4 the situation is more open. And at level 5 the case for establishing separate businesses with multifunctional activities is, as we suggest, almost irresistible.

What, then, does this imply for the management of those sites where extremely large concentrations of manufacturing facilities are in fact to be found? The most obvious thing to explore is the possibility, particularly where different product-ranges are handled in different spatial areas, of dividing responsibilities amongst level 4 representatives of different and distinct operating companies, each of which undertakes its own marketing and product-development functions, as well as manufacturing ones (see Figure 10.1). Such across-site activities as do absolutely demand unified control – provision of an integrated transport service perhaps, or concern for common security arrangements – may be handled by one of the several production chiefs concerned, acting with co-ordinating authority as regards his or her colleagues. But no 'site director' is then needed – not at least, one with an overall main-managerial role.

Behind this lies, however, a more fundamental question: why have

Figure 10.1 Possible split of responsibilities on super-large production sites

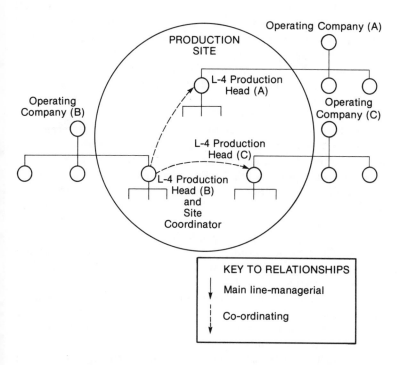

such large sites in the first place? Are considerations of effective *social* organisation being ignored in the interests of economies of scale? Are the imperatives of technology really so powerful?

Regional and Area Structures in Commercial Services

A second area where, in our experience, management structures seem regularly to go awry is to be found in banking, insurance and allied fields. Any large bank or insurance company is faced with the problem of managing dozens, hundreds, or even thousands of local branches, scattered widely throughout the country. Some sort of intermediate structure is needed between top management and the heads of local branches. But what should it be?

In several cases which we have had the chance to examine and discuss, a two-tier structure has developed: branches grouped into areas under area managers, area managers grouped into regions under regional managers (or the like). But even superficial investigations expose considerable doubts about the real function of these intermediate levels. Nowadays, the design of new services or products (insurance policies or investment schemes, for example) is tackled centrally. So is most, if not all, of the development of detailed methods of handling enquiries, cash, and information, through sophisticated data-processing equipment. An elaborate system of central experts provide advice on specialised fields of business. There is a necessary visiting and checking function to be carried out, but much of this might be achieved through a separate inspectorate or audit system, outside any line-management structure. What of real substance is left for a so-called area or regional manager in a line role?

The essential starting point in any consideration of intermediate management structure must be an analysis of the level or levels of work expected of the branches themselves. Our own explorations, so far as they have gone, would lead us to assume that there is not just one possible answer here but several. Many typical branches will call for a head at level 3 – somebody who, in terms of internal matters, can run the whole unit in a systematic way making the best possible use of all available people, equipment and facilities; and in terms of external matters, can respond adequately to those clients or customers, often working in other institutions, whose own problems are of level 3 complexity. There may well, however, be smaller branches where a level 2 head is all that can be justified or afforded – a working manager with a small handful of assistants. At the other extreme, in larger city-centres for example, heads of branch at level 4 may be called for in view of the extreme complexity of the work presented by customers.

If this picture is realistic, then it has profound implications for higher structure. To revert to the general case for a moment, there are, as we have seen in previous chapters, strong arguments against putting people under managers who operate either at the same broad work level, or (apart from personal secretaries or assistants) at two or more steps removed. The optimum for both good personal relationships and effective working is exactly one work-level distance.

In the particular case at issue here what might be called for, therefore, would be the sort of structure shown in Figure 10.2. Heads of level 2 branches are brought together under a number of 'group managers' (or whatever) at level 3 whose job it is to provide the systematic framework in which the former may best operate. But such group managers cannot hope to play an effective management role in relation to any branch managers who themselves work at level 3. The latter will naturally be looking for a boss at level 4, and may possibly be brought together under some regional manager (or whatever) at this higher level. Such a regional manager might also act as an appropriate level of boss for any group managers working in the same locality. However, heads of any level 4 branches in the region could not, by the same arguments, be brought directly under a regional manager at this level (although the latter might possibly play some co-ordinating role on a regional basis, where regional integration appeared for any reason important). An appropriate boss for level 4 branch managers would need to operate at a higher level still, level 5, and might well be identified amongst general management at headquarters.

Figure 10.2

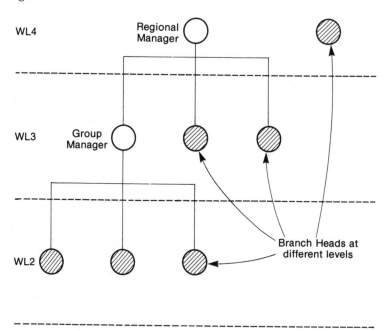

Before leaving this topic, at least one alternative possibility is worthy of remark. One insurance company which we came across appeared to have no line-management levels whatsoever between its general manager and its forty or so branch heads. One set of headquarters departments controlled the actual content of insurance work, whilst another set of departments dealt with personnel and other supporting services. Assuming that the chief executive of this £500 million turnover company was working at least at level 5, and that most of the branch managers were working (as seemed indicated) at level 3, this seemed a case where, far from having too many levels of management, there were actually foo few. The consequence (as far as limited discussion could establish) was that one whole essential layer of work – the comprehensive development and provision of given ranges of service – was being neglected, or dealt with at best in a piecemeal fashion.

Top Structures in Multinationals

In discussions with senior executives from several large multinational organisations, we have come across another problem of top structures on which work-level ideas throw a new light. The situation is one which commonly arises where a world-wide corporation groups its various operating companies in several major continental blocks – one for North America say, one for Europe, and so on – and then further divides them into a variety of sub-regions – Britain and Scandinavia, France and Germany, and so on. The common problem reported is a lack of distinct roles, an experience of executives at regional, subregional and operating company level all struggling for a share of the same area of decision-making.

The root of the problem seems to be this: *larger territory alone does not in itself imply a higher work level.* The higher level only emerges when work of some qualitatively different and broader kind is demanded. (In a sense, this is a repeat of the issue just examined in looking at geographical structures at a lower level in banking and insurance.) If our theories about work levels above level 5 are correct (and we stressed their tentative nature when describing them) the situation should be viewed as follows. Assuming that basic operating companies are themselves at level 5 – an assumption which would require careful testing in any given case – the next thing is to identify some higher-level holding companies at level 7 which are responsible for developing the appropriate 'meta-fields', whatever they are, and regardless for the moment of the geographical span involved.

As described in Chapter 3, where particular operating companies are producing things like audio-visual equipment, domestic appliances, electrical generators, transformers, and so on, the appropriate meta-field might be simply 'engineering'. For any concerned, say, with fast-food chains, cinema, travel agencies, and so on, the meta-field might be 'leisure services'. Given such a differentiation of functions (and leaving to one side for the moment level 6 work), there would be no question of executives at the two different levels being forced any more to fight over the same ground. The essential job of the level 5 executives would be to provide and develop services in their own particular fields. The essential job of the level 7 executives would be to review performance and to consider where new level 5 operating companies were needed or where existing ones should be restructured or run down.

However, there would be room (if the theory is right) for a level between the two with its own characteristic work, level 6. Any intermediate groupings at this level would, as described earlier, have the essential job of running particular conglomerations of level 5 operting units – co-ordinating their activities, adjudicating on boundary issues, allocating finance, approving capital projects, and so on. And this is a level which could readily be formed from aggregations of operating companies in the same line of business across a multiplicity of territories – all the fast-food chain operators in Western Europe, for example.

As regards this particular issue of top structuring, then, the conclusion would seem to be as follows. Above operating companies at level 5 there may be room for one level of executive organisation which consists of simple geographical aggregations of like units, but there is probably not room for more than one. At higher levels still, it is essential, if management-levels are not to be duplicated, to have some definition of a new and greater area of business activity, some given meta-field which is to be systematically covered and developed.

Summary

In looking at top structures in industry and commerce we have considered three areas where special problems seem regularly to arise: very large manufacturing sites; territorial division in country-wide commercial services; and broader regional groupings in multinational corporations. We do not for a moment assume that these are the only, or prime, areas of problem. They are merely those that happen to have come to our own attention in recent years of work.

The only common message is the basic one cited at the start of the chapter: without due regard for optimum numbers of levels and the precise quality of work expected from each, management structures tend to get cluttered and clogged: people fight for the same decision-making ground, and sense of personal responsibility weakens, effectiveness and morale both go down.

The view which we have taken of this particular field is, then, a partial one. But the examples quoted demonstrate how the design approach applies here, too, and the sort of insights and prospects for practical improvement which it offers.

11 Top Structures in Health Services and Local Government

In this chapter various applications of the design approach to top structures in health services and local government are described. As in the previous chapter, 'top structure' is taken to correspond to work level 4 upward. (Discussion of lower levels of work in such public services has already taken place in Chapters 8 and 9.) On the health side we draw upon explorations in field projects and workshops undertaken by ourselves and colleagues with many thousands of senior people from the National Health Service (officers, clinicians and authority members); and also with numbers of senior officers of the Department of Health and Social Security. On the local authority side, we draw upon explorations at different times with the top officers of most Social Services Departments in the country; various contacts with the senior staff of Housing and Education Departments; and two separate pieces of work with the whole chief-officer groups of a London borough and a large non-metropolitan district respectively.[1]

Whilst there are distinct differences between health services and local government there are also important similarities. In both cases there is a running problem of how best to draw together under effective general management a variety of diverse, strongly professionalised groupings. And in both cases there is the fundamental question of the best size and shape of the basic service-delivering entity (the individual local authority or health authority) and just what kind or level of output it is supposed to provide.

Top Structural Problems in Health Services
Since the formation of the British National Health Service in 1948 three major structural issues have been in continual evidence, each giving rise to its own characteristic cluster of problems. The first and most fundamental has been (as just described) the proper size and kind of basic service-providing entity at local level. The second has been the best internal structure to allow ample scope for independent pro-

fessional practice and development (particularly in respect of medicine itself) whilst simultaneously maintaining some effective system of general management. The third has been the proper role of central and regional authorities *vis-à-vis* health authorities at local level; and, more specifically, whether regional authorities are necessary at all. Work-level and related ideas cast a strong light on each and every one of these issues, as we now demonstrate.

The Form of the Basic Health-Service Entity

With a huge enterprise like the NHS, employing nearly one million people, there is an obvious limit to the number of things that can be dealt with centrally. The way in which services are organised at local level has a profound effect on the output actually delivered and the way it does or does not develop. But how should the local health-service-delivery entities be formed? What should they look like?

In the original 1948 organisation of the NHS, responsibility for local provision was split among a variety of different authorities – Boards of Governors (for teaching hospitals), Hospital Management Committees (for others), Local Executive Councils (for family practitioner services) and Public Health Departments. Some of these agencies perhaps achieved a level 5 impact; most a level 4 one, and some, probably only a level 3 one.

In the 1974 reorganisation a major attempt was made to overcome this fragmentation and diversity of approach, Area Health Authorities were established with remits which spanned health services of all kinds, hospital and community, specialist and general. To facilitate co-operation between their respective services, a decision was taken to make the new Area Health Authorities exactly coterminous with existing local authorities. But herein lay another problem. The natural population size of a basic health unit capable of providing a reasonably comprehensive range of health services, but still in good touch with its own locality and its own practitioners, was calculated at around a quarter of a million. Many of the then existing local authorities were, however, very much bigger. Having opted for co-terminosity, the only possible resort seemed to be to break large Area Health Authorities into smaller operating units, to be headed not by further statutory authorities, but by small teams of officers and clinicians, called District Management Teams. The latter, supposedly at least, were accountable not to the corresponding teams of officers at Area level, but directly to the Area Health Authorities themselves.[2]

As became obvious in practice, this last split between District and Area levels in larger authorities was at best ambiguous and at worst highly disruptive. Work-level analysis pinpointed the problem: just who was supposed to be undertaking the level 5 work? Our own investigations at the time showed that in some multi-district authorities it tended to be the area officers, with district officers happy to stay at level 4. In others, each district team took its own firm grip on level 5 work, with area officers falling back more or less resignedly, into the role of referees and coordinators. In many others again, a fierce battle raged in effect for who was to command the level 5 heights, Area or District staff.

In a further series of major reforms introduced in 1982, the Area-District distinction was abolished. Coterminosity with local authorities was abandoned as a binding rule, and newly-named District Health Authorities were established in various shapes and sizes. In terms of population, most were around a quarter of a million, but some were as small as eighty or ninety thousand. Below District level a new substructure of 'Units' was introduced, each comprising perhaps one major hospital, or a group of smaller hospitals, or all mental health services, or all community services. Each Unit was to plan its own services and hold its own budgets, and it was emphasized that Unit officers were directly subordinate to their District counterparts, not to some intermediate management tier (but not to the statutory Authority either). The aim – a laudable one – was to push many decisions closer to the patient: to involve clinicians more fully in management; and to speed up the decision-making process.[3]

In practice the establishment of effective Units of this kind turned out to be far from easy. Some Districts more or less managed it. But in others, senior staff in many if not all of the new Units were left wondering at the end of the day just how much had really changed, just what new powers they really possessed. If specific plans or expenditure proposals were developed, these usually had still to go to District level for checking or ratification. The actual decision process seemed as long and confused as ever.

From substantial fieldwork in four Districts, together with work-shop discussion with senior staff from over one hundred others, the following analysis emerged.[4] In many or most Districts the genuine possibility did arise of delegating full level 4 responsibility and authority to Unit officers and teams. Indeed, this could be seen as amounting to a positive requirement where the Unit concerned was a large general hospital with its own spontaneous programme of clinical innovation. With such a level 4 brief, Unit teams, including clinical representatives, should be expected and allowed to settle their own internal priorities and to develop their own comprehensive and costed plans rather than just producing streams of *ad hoc* suggestions, or bids for cash or staff. They should be allowed not only to hold their own budgets for most if not all activities, but also (what gives real meaning to 'budget holding') to exercise at their own discretion some significant degree of virement; that is, the redeployment of money between various budget heads according to contingencies met during the year. They should be expected to review and control all expenditure, not just that arising in isolated areas like overtime or travel payments, or materials costs (as often happens in level 3 work). In brief, the new Units should be allowed and expected at all time to take a comprehensive view of needs and possibilities within their own domains, both long- and short-term, although always within guidelines laid down from above.

In order to achieve all this, however, several stringent conditions would have to be met. For a start, each Unit should be a natural entity for comprehensive planning. (A so-called elderly unit, for example, which covered only specialist geriatric hospitals and ignored the numerous services for the elderly being provided in general hospitals, mental institutions, community services, and so on, would not provide an adequate framework for level 4 work.) Secondly, each Unit should be big enough to allow the appointment of top staff of sufficient number and grade to make a level 4 approach a real possibility. Thirdly, each Unit should have its own separate source of financial support and advice.

Given a genuine delegation of level 4 work to Units, it should then become possible for District officers (or at least one or more key ones) to start to operate properly at level 5. (We assume, as discussed in Chapter 5, that governing bodies do not operate at a higher work level than top executive officers, but act in a complementary mode, setting or sanctioning all major policies.[5]) The level 5 task would include considering what specific ranges of concrete services to provide over the coming years; which services to leave to other agencies whether public, private or voluntary; and which services to run down or omit altogether. It would include establishing the shape, tasks and boundaries of specific Units, and deciding or proposing specific divisions of resources between them. It would include the vetting of detailed Unit plans and expenditure proposals for conformity to District policy and standards (though not the detailed reworking of any unsatisfactory proposals).

This, then, is how, in most Districts at least, the general idea of pushing decisions closer to the patient could be given a concrete manifestation. Over the course of several years we in fact helped four different Health Districts, two of large and two of medium size, to implement this particular model in detail.

It became obvious in workshop discussions, however, that there were certain Districts in which, because of their very small size, such a model would be completely unrealistic. Such very small Districts were comparable in many ways to individual Units in larger authorities. In such cases it would be natural for District-level staff to retain all level 4 work. Whether they also had the time or personal capability to venture into level 5 work would be a matter of chance. In such cases, however, the main point would be that Units could not themselves operate at level 4, at least not without the fundamental conflict that always arises when two successive levels of management are forced to act at the same level of work. All long-term planning and negotiation of across-the-board priorities would have to rest with District staff. They would be the ones to hold the comprehensive budgets and to exercise any necessary virement of money between heads. In this situation, the natural level for Unit officers would be level 3. It would be their job to develop and run effective systems for their particular Units within staff establishments, physical facilities, and expenditure limits which were effectively set by higher management. (This second model raises, of course, the broader question of the acceptability of having certain Districts operating at a different and lower level than others – a matter to which we will return.)

Internal Management Structure in Health Services
Particular difficulty in creating strong management structures in hospital and other health services appears to arise in all developed societies. One major stumbling block is the considerable power and autonomy inevitably exercised by the leading doctors (an issue already noted in Chapter 9). A second is the existence of a wide range of other developed professions – nurses, physiotherapists, occupational therapists, psychologists and so on – each demanding, with some justification, its own independent voice in top deliberations.

By way of response to these realities, in the 1974 reorganisation, much emphasis was placed on the need for teamworking at top levels, including the regular involvement of elected medical representatives. But in the event, so-called 'consensus management' was judged in many places to be indecisive and long-winded. In the effort to get crisper leadership and clearer accountability following the Griffiths Report of 1983, the further step was taken of introducing a new breed of general managers at Unit, District and Regional levels.[6] This, however, proved to give rise to a new batch of difficulties and uncertainties including such crucial questions as the exact authority that a general manager could be expected to wield over medical consultants and heads of other professions, and whether or not there would still be a need for some kind of teamwork.

In many discussions with top health service managers and clinicians the following analysis emerged. In Units in which in reality only level 3 work was possible (Figure 11.1(a)) a level 4 general manager would clearly be out of place. But any level 3 general manager (if such a title is not already a contradiction in terms) within such a Unit would inevitably find himself or herself working alongside many other staff at the same level – senior nursing managers, all the senior clinicians, principal paramedical heads, and so on. There would thus be no space for any main line-managerial relationships (as earlier defined) with such people, only a monitoring and co-ordinating relationship of greater or lesser strength. A standing management team might or might not be formed from amongst the various level 3 heads, but most system-development work (the top level of work in such a Unit) would be pursued by *ad hoc* interactions amongst the particular senior staff involved in any issue in question.

There would be some similarities between level 4 Units and level 4 Districts (Figure 11.1(b)). Any Unit really capable of being run at level 4 would be likely to need, as well as a general manager at this level, a level 4 head nurse (in view of the sheer size of the nursing operation) and one or more doctors to represent the medical staff, also capable of thinking and working at level 4. Any level 4 District would certainly need a treasurer, a chief nurse and perhaps an administrative medical officer capable of work at this level, as well again as level 4 representatives of medical staff. In neither case (if the hypothesis of one main management role per work level is right) could the general manager therefore expect to develop a complete main line-managerial relationship to other key colleagues. In both cases it would be essential to create or retain a top team, in order to develop corporate and comprehensive plans and expenditure proposals. In such a team the general manager could play a strong chairman role, with monitoring and co-ordinating authority, but no more.

In level 5 Districts (Figure 11.1(c)), the general manager might certainly want his or her own subordinate staff at level 4: a chief planner, a personnel director, a director of administration, or whatever. If heads of other main functions like nursing, medical administration and finance also operated at level 4 then (leaving aside doctors) something like a straightforward managerial hierarchy might thus be possible. Various teams and deliberative groups might be established, in all of which the general manager would naturally act as chairman. However, there might well be a strong imperative, particularly in larger and more complex Districts, to have officers other than the general managers – treasurers for example – who were also capable of operating at level 5. And in any event it would certainly be hoped to

Figure 11.1 Various possible management relationships in Health Service Districts and their Units

(a) In level 3 units

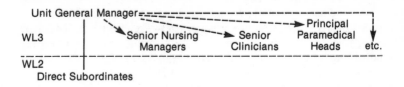

(b) In level 4 units or level 4 districts

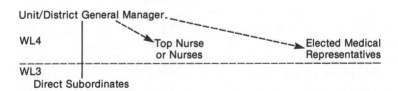

(c) In level 5 districts

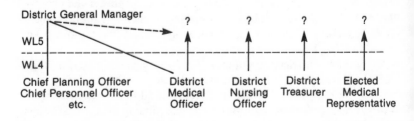

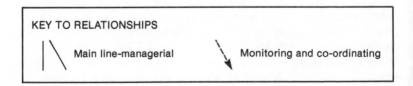

attract into top management discussions leading medical representatives capable of thinking at this level – people whose primary line of
responsibility would be directly to those who elected them, rather than
to the general manager. Thus, although in relation to most of the
senior staff the general manager would carry main line-managerial
authority, in relation to at least a few others he or she could here again
carry no more than monitoring and co-ordinating authority of some
greater or lesser range.

Generally then, as regards management structures in a health
service, a work-level analysis suggests that however much status or
weight is given to one leading executive figure, and however much
might change in terms of managerial *style*, that something more
complex than a straightforward industrial-type hierarchy is always
likely to be necessary. (Any realistic analysis of the autonomy of senior
doctors, touched upon in Chapter 5, adds further weight to this
conclusion.)

The Proper Role of Central and Regional Health Authorities

Since the formation of the National Health Service, and particularly
since the creation of comprehensive health authorities at local level,
there has been continual criticism of the part played by Regional
Authorities and, indeed, frequent questionings of the very need for
such bodies. Criticism has also been frequently levelled at the central
health authority – the Department of Health and Social Security – for
the way in which it too constantly intrudes into quite detailed management matters at local level.

It seems a fair presumption that level 7 work in respect of an
organisation the size of the NHS, employing, as we say, getting on for
one million people, needs to be done somewhere. The obvious place
for such work is central government (we will bypass the discussion as
to how it might best be divided amongst ministers, career civil
servants, and others). If the conception of level 7 work (advanced in
Chapter 3) is right, its essence in this case is surveying the metafield of
health or health cum social security, not only to create or reshape the
kinds of agency necessary to provide actual diagnostic and treatment
services for the unwell (that is, actual 'health services'), but to respond
adequately to all the other multitudinous factors that bear one way or
another on the health of the individual and community.

On the assumption that most if not all District Health Authorities
are expected to operate at level 5, it then follows that there is need for
an intermediate level 6 structure of some kind. If the conception of
level 6 work (also advanced in Chapter 3) is right, the essential activity
is dealing with particular complexes of level 5 agencies – in this case

neighbouring District Authorities – so as to ensure that the fields concerned are covered in a co-ordinated and balanced fashion. Exactly how this is best organised in the context of the NHS takes us into deeper water, although on the assumption (a) that the people carrying out such work need to be in reasonably close physical proximity to the Health Districts concerned, and (b) that final value judgements about social needs and priorities in this field need to be made by elected or appointed public representatives rather than employed officers, then something like the present system of Regional Authorities does inevitably emerge.

Various discussions with regional staff of the NHS and with staff of the Department of Health and Social Security have confirmed the following analysis of what are, and are not, appropriate activities for Regional and Central authorities operating at level 6 and level 7 respectively. Appropriate work for Regional Authorities operating at level 6 would include such things as setting particular *regional* strategies and priorities (so as to forward nationally-set policies); making differential assessments of the depth and strength of under-lying health needs in the various subordinate Districts; and allocating finance and other scarce resources accordingly (having allowed for any regional or sub-regional services run by particular Districts). Appropriate work for a central authority operating at level 7 would include such things as setting any necessary *national* strategies (for example on major reorganisations or training programmes); making differential assessments of the needs of various *Regions*; and allocating finance and other scarce resources accordingly to Regional Authorities (allowing for any cross-regional services). It can be taken that at both regional and central levels there are also the common management tasks in relation to the next level down (in each case) of setting general organisational frameworks; attending to the appoint-ment of key personnel; monitoring plans for adherence to higher policy; and reviewing actual performance.

It is already generally accepted that neither the central health authority nor Regional Authorities should be directly providing operational services in any significant degree. If in fact Districts are to work fully at level 5 and the higher authorities are to restrict themselves to levels 6 and 7, then it is up to the former, acting within national and regional guidelines, to decide exactly what operational services to provide and how best to provide them. Arguably, higher authorities should not even be initiating specific operational develop-ments, let alone getting involved in their detailed planning or design. However, on these same assumptions, it certainly is part of the role of Regional Authorities (in particular) to be keeping a constant eye on what Districts are actually doing, and more particularly (as suggested above) to be vetting all existing or proposed activities for conformity to national and regional policy.

One of the specific problems in settling an appropriate role for Regional Authorities is that many Districts do not themselves carry out effective level 5 work. In some cases (as already discussed) they are simply too small. Even for those Districts fully equipped for Level 5 work, many fail to carry this out because their top officers are fully occupied with level 4 work, having failed to delegate it effectively to subordinate Units. The upshot is that Regional officers are themselves driven to undertake necessary level 5 work in respect of certain Districts as well as carrying out the requisite level 6 work looking at the Region overall. But this is not at all easy. It is always difficult to maintain two distinct levels of response to subordinate bodies supposedly identical; and it is awkward, to say the least, to have to provide the additional staff and facilities necessary to operate at the lower level as well as the higher one.

In summary as regards health services, then, the design approach indicates possible practical resolutions to many of the most critical organisational issues. It questions whether all present District Authorities are able in fact to operate at level 5. It identifies the choice between (sub-District) Units at level 3 and level 4, spelling out the detailed implications in each case. It poses a specific range of appropriate level 7 activities for the central authority and of appropriate level 6 activities for Regional Authorities. It brings into clear view the equivocal position of the latter in relation to Districts which are not themselves capable of level 5 work. It offers complex, but realistic, models of the different possible authority relationships in general-manager posts.

The Basic Local Authority Entity

Turning now to local authorities, one of the most important issues of structure here, as in health services, is that of the best size, shape and composition of the basic service-delivering entities. Is there a case for a two-tiered structure of Districts and counties (or boroughs and metro-politan authorities), or should these be merged into a single line of 'all-purpose' authorities? If the first, what range of functions should be provided at the lower level and what at the higher, and how might the split between the two be overcome? And what, in either case, is the optimum size of the average Unit so as to make the best balance between efficiency (usually assumed to increase with size) and democratic responsiveness (usually assumed to decrease with size)?

The history of local government reform in British may be seen as a series of attempts, more or less distorted by simple party-political considerations, to come to terms with these prime issues. We ourselves have not had the opportunity to tackle them directly in project work. But a work-level analysis casts new light on many of them.

The most basic question which arises for any service-providing local authority is, it may be suggested, the kind or quality of impact on environment which it is required to make. There are actually two issues: the quality of impact expected of any one constituent department or agency – education, social services, housing, police, works or whatever – and the quality of impact expected of the local authority as a whole. Historically, local authorities have varied enormously in both regards. (One of the motives behind the various national reorganisations that have taken place over the years has, no doubt, been to deal with just this situation.) Many of the authorities of the past (some of the old rural and urban districts, and the smaller boroughs, for example) probably produced overall, no more than a level 3 response. By contrast, our work with various of the post-1974 authorities suggest that many of the individual departments within them, let alone authorities as a whole, were by this time operating at level 4 or 5.

In principle there appears to be the following range of possibilities. (Again we assume that the level of response of an authority as a whole is the level of work carried out by its chief executive officer or officers, and that the task of the governing bodies is different.[7]) Individual departments or services might conceivably be expected to make a level 3, level 4 or level 5 response to their environments. (Less than 'systematic provision' would be hardly believable: more than 'field coverage' would go beyond the conception of one individual department or service.) Authorities as a whole might conceivably be expected to make a level 4, a level 5 or a level 6 response to their environments. (Less than 'comprehensive provision' to any locality would surely be unacceptable: more than 'multi-field coverage' would probably indicate something beyond local government as normally conceived.[8]) Some of the features and relative merits of these various possibilities are considered in the following sections.

General Management Structures in Local Authorities

In local government, as in health services, there has been continual effort over the years to develop in authorities of all kinds more effective structures of internal management. Within local government there has been particular concern with the fragmentation resulting from separate legal duties, committee structures and departments of professional staff. In the effort to do something about this on the lines of the Maud and Bains Reports, a major step was taken in the early 1970s in introducing a new post of chief executive.[9] This innovation, however, proved far from straightforward. Some authorities actually changed their minds after a few years of trial, and abandoned the idea altogether. Our own contacts with many departmental heads have revealed frequent doubts about the proper role of chief executives where (as in most cases) such posts continue to exist, and just how far their authority should run. Discussions suggest the following analysis.

In the case both of level 4 authority with level 4 departments (see Figure 11.2(b)) and a level 5 authority with level 5 departments (see Figure 11.2(d)), there can be no room for a main line-managerial relationship between chief executive and departmental heads. Indeed, it is debatable whether the term 'chief executive' has any real substance in either case. Such a post, though it may be marked in each case by a somewhat higher grade and status than that of other chief officers, is not in these circumstances different in essence from that filled by the traditional town clerk who, as well as providing legal and administrative services, exerted a general monitoring and co-ordination of things such as staffing, accommodation and common procedures. In all such cases, the machinery for substantial cross-departmental coordination of outputs is relatively weak.

In the case where a chief executive is appointed who *is* expected to work at a significantly higher level than departmental heads, something of more substance can be looked for. Even though departmental heads may still possess (in the interests both of proper democratic control and proper professional development) direct access to committees and committee chairmen, so that simple and unconditional main line-management by a chief executive is still impossible, the latter may now play an important and distinctive role. A much stronger integration of outputs as well as inputs now becomes possible.

In an authority with departmental heads at level 3 and a chief executive at level 4 (Figure 11.2(a)), it is up to the latter to ensure the provision of a comprehensive range of services of at least conventional or established types across the whole authority. Individual heads are expected to run their own departments systematically within given staffing and facilities, but no more. In an authority with departmental heads at level 4 and a chief executive at level 5 (Figure 11.2(c)) it is up to each of the former to ensure comprehensive provisions within their own areas. The job of the chief executive (difficult though this may be in view of the extreme diversity of the fields of activity in question) is to do the prime work with regard to the definition or redefinition of required ranges of service in each particular field.

Figure 11.2 Various possible management relationships in local authorities

(a) Level 4 authorities with level 3 departments

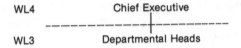

(b) Level 4 authorities with level 4 departments

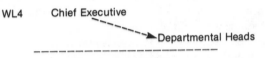

(c) Level 5 authorities with level 4 departments

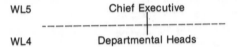

(d) Level 5 authorities with level 5 departments

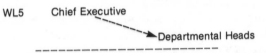

(e) Level 6 authorities with level 5 departments

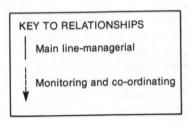

In an authority with departmental heads at level 5 and a chief executive at level 6 (Figure 11.2(e)) it is up to each of the former to provide adequate provision and development within their own particular fields. The job of the chief executive is to ensure adequate coverage of the multi-field complex as a whole. Though this is a demanding task, it is by no means an impossible one. One example which we have come across of such level 6 work was that being done by a chief executive who, amongst other things, was busily developing a co-ordinated strategy for dealing with a run-down area within the locality of this local authority: a strategy involving integrated developments in planning, housing, social services, and recreation.

Common management problems arise in all these models from discrepancies in size between departments: differences between big departments like education, social services and housing, and small ones like leisure, environmental health, or consumer protection. The theory, or practice, of grouping departments into 'directorates' to form an intermediate management tier between the chief executive and individual departmental heads probably flows from attempts to deal with just this situation, although it is often stated to be a response to over-large spans of control (see earlier remarks on the common obsession with spans of control in Chapter 5). If some departments do indeed operate at one or more work levels lower than others, then there is a genuine management gap to be filled. But detailed project work in one authority illustrated the predictable stresses and personal tensions which followed because the directorate system which was in being, attempted at certain points to put heads of major departments under directorate heads who, though more highly paid and graded, operated at the same broad work level.

To sum up as regards local authorities, the design approach affords insights on a number of substantial issues. It offers a new way of describing the scope of exisiting or possible authorities, not just in terms of 'efficiency' but in terms of the quality of impact on the local environment expected from the authority as a whole, or any one of its constituent departments. And it offers a new way of exploring existing or possible management structures, with more realistic descriptions of exactly what might be expected both of so-called chief executives and directorate heads.

Public Services in General

Our analysis of health services and local government leads to a general conclusion of considerable social importance. This is the desirability of having level 5 agencies at local levels in a whole variety of public service fields (this links with the general case for separate level 5 operating units with their own governing systems discussed in Chapter 6).

The arguments for such a stance can be rapidly summarised. In its own particular field, whatever that may be, the public agency capable of a level 5 output or response is the most fully developed operational unit, the one with the widest operational brief. It is certainly possible to establish public agencies which are only expected to operate at level 4, that is, with briefs to provide (or to co-ordinate the provision of) some predetermined range of concretely specified types of service. But, by setting a level 5 brief, the way lies open for a much more creative response: for the continuing development of services of new kinds in some generally defined area of need. In moving from level 4 to level 5, the challenge is, for example, to think fundamentally about basic health-service needs and best ways of responding to them rather than simply providing more hospitals, surgeons, district nurses and so on; or to think in terms of meeting people's lifelong needs for educational services rather than just providing the usual run of primary and secondary teaching; or to consider all kinds of new ways of catering for leisure over and above the straightforward provision of libraries, swimming pools and playing fields.

In suggesting that public-service agencies at local levels should desirably operate at level 5 it is important to stress that this does not necessarily imply that they should directly provide all the services concerned themselves. There is a real choice as to which of all the services needed by any local community should desirably be provided by public agencies and which by voluntary or private ones. The decision is ultimately political: some will favour greater 'municipalisation', some will favour greater 'privatisation'. Having a public agency with a level 5 brief means at least, however, that there is one entity responsible for overviewing the whole scene and providing any necessary co-ordination of activity across the various sectors. (An indication of the sort of thing in mind here is a local authority housing department which provided an advisory service on the availability of housing of all types, private and communally owned as well as local authority-owned, even though the ruling administration of the day were far from being in favour of increased public services in general.)

If the system does not allow level 5 work to be carried out locally, then this particular work either fails to get done at all, or gets forced up to regional or national levels (where it is usually done badly). As people like Donald Schon have argued, the turbulence and complexity of modern life demands individual organisations which are (in his words) 'learning systems ... capable of bringing about their own continuing transformation'.[10] This is simply another way of describing level 5 organisations. Given such self-transforming organisations at the periphery, central government can avoid the fatal delusion that only it can mastermind all significant change, and settle more realistically for a broad regulative and policy-setting role.

To be viable in modern conditions, most level 5 public services probably need to relate to a population of not less than a quarter of a million people. Putting the thing the other way round, at such an order of population it appears possible to establish a full level 5 response in a wide range of services including health, education, welfare and housing (as well, arguably, as others, like police and probation services). In most locations, this implies a territory which can still be easily traversed by either private or public transport where regular visits have to be made to various hospitals, colleges, schools or administrative centres. Thus, at this scale, services may still feel truly local, available 'within the district'. And, moreover, none of these services need be outsize – even a labour-intensive level 5 agency as noted before, should be able to manage on a few thousand staff.

If these various ideas and assumptions are right, then a number of more or less radical possibilities follow. Where, as in Britain, District Health Authorities already exist, effort can be devoted to bringing them all up to full level 5 operation. (Elsewhere the possibility of creating such authorities can be considered.) Generally, more attention can be given to the particular model of local authorities with heads of all major services at level 5 and, perhaps, chief executives at level 6. (Local authority models discussed earlier, where heads of major departments work at level 4, or even level 3, are much less attractive for the reasons just advanced.)

If a population size of roughly a quarter of a million really does permit the possibility of establishing level 5 services in a wide range of fields, then the case for multi-purpose or most-purpose local authorities is strengthened; as is the case for coterminosity of territory between such local authorities and District Health Authorities; perhaps even of an ultimate merger of the two. Such latter steps would not only lead to better-coordinated provision of services, they might also result in the strengthening of each citizen's sense of the particular district in which he or she lives; that is, in the strengthening of the sense of community at a level which, at present, is often so very weak.

Notes

1. See the various references in Chapter 9 to work in the National Health Services, and in local authority Social Services.
2. See the so-called 'Grey Book', Department of Health and Social Security,

Management Arrangements for the Reorganised National Health Service, London, HMSO, 1972.

3. See Department of Health and Social Security, *Patients First*, London, HMSO, 1979; and DHSS Circular HC(80)8, *Health Service Development, Structure and Management*.

4. For further details, see W. Kinston and R. W. Rowbottom, 'The New NHS Districts and Their Units, A Working Paper', Brunel Institute of Organisation and Social Studies, Uxbridge: Brunel University 1983; and W. Kinston, 'District Health Organisation', *Social Policy and Administration*, vol. 18, no. 3, pp. 229–46; see also C. R. Hayton, 'Management Arrangements Below District Level', *Hospital and Health Services Review*, May 1980; and I. Wickings, *Effective Unit Management*, London, King Edward's Hospital Fund, 1983; where, in both cases, work-level ideas are applied to the same topic.

5. Of course the governing bodies of District Health Authorities, like those of Local Authorities or other public agencies, have specific executive functions to carry out as well as setting or sanctioning policies. They must appoint chief officers, review actual performance, take key decisions in planning or resource allocation, and monitor actual outputs in sensitive areas. But we suggest that their work is basically about articulating general community values, preferences and priorities; about saying 'go this direction' or 'go that direction'; at minimum, about *legitimising* the activities of the executive machine. (And, as this last statement implies, officer work is not simply about execution untainted by any policy considerations: officers, particularly the more senior, naturally have their own views on policy, put forward their own policy proposals, and exert their own influence on final decisions.) As noted in Chapter 5, such policy-making or policy-sanctioning work does not necessarily require people of high executive ability. It certainly does not demand a governing body all of whose members are capable of operating one work level higher than the chief officers, as would be the case in a straightforward managerial chain (although there are probably special requirements for chairmen or a few other key figures). Given sensitivity to community issues, and some basic knowledge of the service concerned, people from ordinary walks of life can constitute a perfectly satisfactory rank-and-file membership.

6. See Department of Health and Social Security, *Report on NHS Management Inquiry* (Griffiths Report), London, HMSO, 1983; and *Implementation of the NHS Management Inquiry Report*, DHSS Circuar HC(84)13.

7. See note 5.

8. In each of the possibilities just described, the role of the Local Authority is still seen essentially as that of undertaking a conglomeration of separate though related functions which have been specifically devolved in legislation. There is a broader conception often espoused by enthusiastic exponents of local government, which posits a role for the Local Authority nothing short of that of forwarding the welfare in all respects of the citizens of its locality, freely creating or dissolving new services and new departments as and whenever appears necessary. This is in effect a level 7 response. However, it seems likely that carrying through such work requires a body not just with executive powers but with legislative ones. If so, what is in view is not a Local Authority or local government in the usual sense of these terms, but some form of state or regional government.

9. See Ministry of Housing and Local Government, *Management of Local Government* (Maud Report), London, HMSO, 1967; and *The New Local Authorities, Management and Structure* (Bains Report), London, HMSO, 1972.

10. D.A. Schon, *Beyond the Stable State*, London, Temple Smith, 1971.

12 Conclusion: Uncovering the Practical Options

The design approach which has been described in the previous pages involves ideas of considerable depth and generality. The analysis of authority types in organisation itself offers quite a new slant on leadership (usually conceived solely in terms of personal attributes or styles) and lays the ground for a much more developed science of the structural side of this subject. The work level schema opens still broader vistas. It provides a general description of organised human activity which far transcends, say, modern manufacturing industry or large public services. It throws a new light on the whole nature of hierarchy in human affairs. And it offers the possibility of a radically different method of characterising human abilities.

The approach is thus far from lacking a theoretical dimension. But having said this, if one outstanding feature of this particular approach has to be identified it is, we believe, its *practicality*. It is practical in that (as described at length in previous pages) it is firmly rooted in actual and pressing problems faced by managers and others in a wide variety of organisations. And it is practical in that it is equally firmly orientated towards the effective resolution of such problems. It does not pretend to offer detailed answers in every circumstance (final actions in any case must always be determined by local and specific factors as well as generalisable ones). Nor does it pretend to cover every issue which arises in organisational life, or deal in equal depth with all those which it does address (any approach which claims to be finished and all-comprehending must in any event be suspect). But its range of application is considerable. And its focus is sharp.

In this question of practicality the approach that has been described differs significantly from many others to the same subject. Most current ideas and theories about organisation do not figure at all well against this particular criterion. They give every evidence of originating not from actual problems in the manager's in-tray (so to speak) but from interesting issues in the researcher's mind. Not surprisingly, if they finish up providing anything of value, it is more in the nature of general psychological or sociological insights than direct practical guidance.

Throughout our own work, our constant attempt is to delineate the practical options with maximum clarity and precision; to cut sharply and cleanly; to avoid at all costs the easy cliché, the dubious maxim, the airy circumlocution. Practising managers often have to fudge issues deliberately for very good reasons; but it is never appropriate for the organisation analyst to do so. We may conclude, therefore, by summarising the real and practical options in respect of different aspects of organisation which have been exposed at various point, in the previous text, noting again any vague stereotyped or mythical ideas which commonly obscure them.

Options for Basic Management Structures

For a start, in dealing with problems of typical management hierarchies it is essential, as we have seen, to separate *authority structures* on the one hand from *pay, grading* or *status structures*, on the other, and both from *work levels* (Chapters 2 and 3).

Invariably it is best to begin with a clear understanding of the work to be done. The work level schema, unlike vague phrases such as 'top management', 'middle management' and 'first-level management', allows a precise indication of the expected task of any manager or other practitioner in any organisation, large, medium or small (Chapter 3).

In proceeding to analyse or specify the authority structure itself, it is best to go directly to exact authority types: main line-managerial, supervisory, co-ordinating, monitoring, and so on. Phrases like 'line and staff', 'functional organisation' or 'professional organisation' usually obscure many critical issues. The idea of 'line and staff' in particular carries a great danger of leading to the assumption (a) that those in staff posts carry no authority whatsoever (which is almost invariably wrong), and (b) that all shown or described as 'in line' do in fact carry major or key managerial roles (which is often or usually wrong as well) (Chapter 2).

Any perceived need to distinguish between 'line authority', on the one hand, and 'functional' or 'professional' authority, on the other, is almost certainly indicative of the presence of what we have described as *dual influence*. Situations of the latter type abound in large organisations. The notion of 'unity of command' may serve a rough purpose at times in drawing attention to the desirability of knowing the exact location of main line-managerial roles. But the idea that all necessary commands and instructions in complex organisations could be directed through a single-channel system is plain nonsense. The practical task of dual-influence situations is to specify exactly what elements of authority rest in each line. Occasionally, what can only be described as 'co-management' will appear to be the optimum – the very negation (apparently) of the unity-of-command principle (Chapter 2).

Particular problems undoubtedly arise where *professionals* find themselves subject to, or actually working within, management structures. However a simple appeal to the principle of 'professional autonomy' itself solves nothing and usually serves only to put contending parties in one of two entrenched positions – for it or against it. As we have seen, the whole area of professional organisation cannot be properly understood without considering the various typical steps or levels in professional work, starting at the bottom of work level 2 and progressing to level 3. Given clarity on the exact level or sub-level of work required, most issues of appropriate freedom and control can be resolved in detail and with confidence (though, in some cases, there are additional factors to be taken into account like special relationships to be maintained with patients or clients, or academic freedom) (Chapter 9).

Generally, in structuring managerial hierarchies, the key principle is, as we have seen, only one main line-managerial post for each work level above the first (Chapter 3). The myth of the optimum or maximum span of control still holds, in our experience, a very powerful sway in everyday organisational life (although people find it difficult, when pressed, to say exactly what the optimal number actually is). In fact, any obsession with small spans usually has disastrous consequences for management levels, causing far too many to be created or attempted. Where excessive spans (whatever they may be) do appear to be arising, the appropriate answer, as we have seen, is to create *staff officers* or *supervisors* to aid in the management process; not to try and force in more main line-managers (Chapter 5).

Having decided the most fundamental question in management structures, which is the expected work level in various jobs, it is possible to address *pay, grading or status* matters. Again, the main thing is to distinguish these clearly from authority relationships. But there may be much to be said, as we have seen, in making an explicit link between any grading structures and underlying work levels. Often, several grades per work level may be required (Chapter 4).

Options in Appointments and Promotions
In considering the filling of particular posts it is necessary, as we have seen, to go beyond vague references to 'competence', 'skill', 'ability',

and so on, and to separate two very different things. First is the basic knowledge or basic expertise required in order to operate in the particular field concerned – engineering, accountancy, medicine, personnel work, or whatever; the *kind* of ability required. Second is the ability to cope with work of a given *level* in the given field – prescribed output, situational response, systematic provision, and so on. All too often, confusion of these two dimensions leads to highly-qualified people being appointed or promoted to jobs they cannot do; or poorly-qualified but otherwise able people being held back from high-level jobs which they might do very well (Chapter 4).

Having a clear conception of level, as well as kind, of ability, also makes it possible to draft more-precise advertisements for staff; to have a clearer conception of what qualities to look for in interviews with applicants; and to have a better sense of the difference between current and potential abilities (Chapter 4).

Options in Specifying Expected Impact on Envionment
Generally, the work level schema allows a better fix to be made on each and every job in the organisation. But it has particular significance in relation to 'front-line' jobs at one end and chief executive jobs at the other.

It is no good just talking about 'highly-responsive' or 'innovative' organisations (Chapter 6). Definite choices need to be made about the *basic expected work level* at the front line. This is, in many cases, where service is directly provided to individual customers or clients. Here, the choice is usually between levels 1, 2 and 3. Equally if not more important choices need to be made about the *highest expected work level*, the level of effective impact of the organisation as a whole on its total environment, society or community (a level which equates to the expected work in the chief executive post or posts). For any single operating organisation or division, the usual choice here will be between levels 3, 4 or 5; but larger complexes may be required to make a level 6 or even level 7 impact (Chapter 5).

Options for Division or Grouping
The main options in principle for dividing up or grouping activities at any given level are by *place, time, clientele, function, product or service*, and *project or programme*. No one is best, though certain are more feasible at particular work levels then others (Chapter 5).

Whatever the prime basis of division chosen at any level, the demands of other bases can never be completely ignored. The likely result is some form of organisation in two or more dimensions, that is, some form of *matrix organisation* (Chapter 5).

Options for Teamwork, Matrix Organisation, Decentralisation and Greater Participation

When problems are pervasive and dissatisfaction looms large, the need is sometimes voiced for a radically different form of organisation. However, as we have seen, ideas like 'non-bureaucratic', 'organic', 'open-system' or 'polyarchic' organisation are far too big and vague in themselves to resolve specific practical problems or to provide specific design guidance. Very often, in any case, the real demand may be for a change in *managerial style* or *culture*. Where structural change itself is required, however, general terms like those just described are simply not enough. Detailed consideration is alway needed of exactly how new management structures are to operate; on what basis any additional teams, working parties, or councils are to work; exactly who is accountable for making what sort of response to environmental needs and circumstances; where authority is ultimately to rest; and so on. Whatever else is changed, differences in levels of work to be done will always remain (Chapter 6).

Teamwork is undoubtedly a vital ingredient in all successful organisation. But neither the identification of particular bodies nor a general cry for 'more teamwork' is enough on its own. Much more specificity is needed. For a start, teamwork in practice by no means always implies (as it is often assumed to do) complete equality amongst membership. As we have seen, various models of internal authority structure are possible, and conflict and confusion may often result if it is not made clear which is to prevail. As always, appropriate authority relations will be much influenced by the work levels (the same or different) at which various members are expected to operate (Chapter 6).

Matrix organisation, too, is a broad type, not an exact practical model. 'Dual-influence' situations are one inevitable consequence. There are tricky questions of authority relationship to be negotiated, with many alternatives in principle. Again, any distinctions in work level amongst the various parties involved are likely to be crucial (Chapter 6).

Any call for *decentralisation* (like that for more teamwork) without further detailing is an empty gesture. In making decentralisation a reality, a clear definition of work levels is again crucial. Each different work level demands in fact its own appropriate kind of delegated authority and control. The term 'divisionalisation' is best kept for self-contained units at level 4 and above, with their own separate tasks and finances. In very large organisations the establishment of separate level 5 operating units with their own distinct field of work and governing bodies is one of the most important steps to effective decentralisation (Chapter 6).

Greater *participation* is another admirable sentiment which, unaccompanied by detailed systems and structures, can easily amount to nothing. Arguably, the most important thing in getting people to participate is ensuring that each has a job of a kind and level which stretches his or her particular talents to the full. Beyond this are two main possibilities, significantly different and distinct. The first is the development of specific arrangements to enable all at any given level to participate in major executive decision-making at the next work level up. The second is the development of more general systems to let all in a given organisation participate in some way in its overall governance, crossing all work levels (Chapter 6).

A Final Word

Any complete science of organisation must be multi-layered. At deeper points it must connect with general political and social thought and the broader fields of psychology and individual development. At middle levels there is room for it to develop more specific concepts and theories of its own. But ultimately, given after all that organisations of the kind in focus are purpose-built entities with specific practical aims, any science of organisation worth its name should be able to furnish concrete, practical guidance.

The approach described in this book does, as we have noted, develop specific concepts and theories. And it does offer connection of various kinds with broader social and psychological ideas. But above all, it offers direct practical help, and help, moreover, of a tried and tested kind – *it actually works*. We hope that many readers will now be in a position to try it out for themselves.

Index